Gaston County

NORTH CAROLINA

Gaston County

NORTH CAROLINA

A BRIEF HISTORY

Rita Wehunt-Black

THE
History
PRESS

Published by The History Press
Charleston, SC 29403
www.historypress.net

First published 2008

ISBN 978.1.5402.1805.6

Library of Congress Cataloging-in-Publication Data

Wehunt-Black, Rita.
Gaston County, North Carolina : a brief history / Rita Wehunt-Black.
p. cm.
Includes bibliographical references and index.
ISBN 978-1-5402-1805-6
1. Gaston County (N.C.)--History. I. Title.

F262.G2W46 2008
975.6'773--dc22
2007049553

This book is dedicated to Pat C. Sherrill of Cherryville. Her unrelenting dedication to, passion for and amount of time spent on the preservation of Gaston County history never ceases to amaze and astound me!

Contents

Preface

I've been sifting through the layers
of dusty books and faded papers.
They tell a story…
one that happened so long ago.[1]

I think that I was born a historian. I cut my teeth on books like *The Genealogy of Pieter Heyl and His Descendants*, *Rhinelanders on the Yadkin* and *Our Kin*, while listening to stories about the Civil War from my mother. In high school I carried around *Carolina Cradle* and thought it was the most wonderful book. My love of history and genealogy also started in high school. I knew nothing of mills or mill towns until I was introduced to Liston Pope's *Millhands and Preachers* in 1969 at Gaston College. I thought it was such a powerful book then, and it remains one of my most prized books.

I grew up in Lincoln County, not many miles from the Gaston-Lincoln County line, and although I am not a native of Gaston County, I have been among you. I feel that Gaston County is my home and my heritage as much as Lincoln County, almost as if the division in 1846 never happened. My Dellinger and Craft roots, and my husband's Neal, Black and Alexander roots cut deep into Gaston County.

I have fond memories of visiting a great-aunt in Gastonia and walking from her house to the Webb Theater in the 1950s. I tagged along with my father to Hoffman's Service Station on Franklin Avenue at "Greasy Corner," and as a child my two favorite cocker spaniels came from Dr. Gingles, a veterinarian in Gastonia. Later I married a Gaston County native, graduated from Sacred Heart College in 1973 and lived in Gaston County for many years while teaching.

I have such pleasant memories of my college days at Sacred Heart and Belmont Abbey in Belmont. I still go back at times just to walk on the campuses. They are two of the most serene places in Gaston County, although I have discovered many others in the process of writing this book.

Acknowledgements

So many people helped and inspired me along the way in completing this brief history of Gaston County. Some never knew of the roles they played, like Joe DePriest, whose daily inspiration came in the form of his articles in the *Gaston Observer* each morning, and Flora Ann Scearce, who wrote *Cotton Mill Girl* and whose book signing and reading I attended in August of 2007. Some of those I met while rambling around Gaston County with my camera and notes may never know of their inspiration and help. The kindness and professionalism of people like Aimee Russell at the Gaston County Art and History Museum in Dallas, and the staff at the Gaston-Lincoln Regional Library in Gastonia made it a joy to work with them.

The work and contributions of people like Dr. Alan May, Lucy Penegar and Robert Carpenter, just to name a few, amaze me, and their scholarly works were such a great help in writing this brief history.

I can never adequately thank Lee Handford, commissioning editor at The History Press in Charleston, South Carolina. She knew before I did that I needed to write a book about Gaston County history.

I want to thank both my husband John H. Black Jr. and my sister, Dorothy W. Pearson, the two people in my life who take care of the present so that I may take care of the past.

As you have noticed, I keep using the term "brief history" because there are so many histories, so many stories, so many people and hundreds of photographs that did not make it into this book due to limitations of space. It pained me greatly when I had to eliminate some of these things.

Introduction

Civilization is a stream with banks. The stream is sometimes filled with blood from people killing, stealing, shouting and doing the things historians record, while on the banks, unnoticed, people build homes, make love, raise children, sing songs, write poetry and even whittle statues. The story of civilization is the story of what happens on the banks.

—Will Durant

In this brief narrative and interpretative history of Gaston County, I have tried to include glimpses of the "people on the banks"; people like "the Hat Lady" and the "other Simon Hager," and even some people like Lizzie Michume whose stories I don't yet know.

There have been many beautiful books written on Gaston County—books like Sally Griffin's *Gaston Remembers: Weaving a Tapestry in Time*; Ross Yockey's *Between Two Rivers*; the pictorial *Gastonia and Gaston County, North Carolina* by Piper Peters Aheron; *Bessemer City Centennial, 1893–1993*; and books by Robert A. Ragan, Robert Williams and so many more.

There are quaint and wonderful books that have been around since the 1930s, '40s, '50s and '60s, sort of like old friends of mine, such as Minnie Stowe Puett's *History of Gaston*; Cope and Wellman's *The County of Gaston*; the books by Joseph H. Sepack; and Liston Pope's *Millhands and Preachers*. My hope is that this brief history will inspire you to go out and find these wonderful books and dig deeper into the history of Gaston County and the lives of the people who made it such an interesting place.

So, my friend, I hope to see you soon on the banks of the river, figuratively or literally.

CHAPTER 1

The Lay of the Land

Gaston County is located in the southwestern part of the North Carolina Piedmont. The landscape is mostly rolling hills, but there are also several prominent ridges and smaller mountain ranges. The elevation ranges from 1,705 feet above sea level in the southwest at the pinnacle of the Kings Mountain Range to 587 feet in the southeast corner of the county. Two reservoirs, Mountain Island Lake and Lake Wylie, have been created on the Catawba River. Gaston County is dominated by tributaries of the Catawba River. Wide flood plains occur along both the South Fork and the Catawba. Springs are abundant throughout the county.[2]

The Natural Heritage Inventory of Gaston County, North Carolina is a fascinating four-page executive summary report that identifies and lists thirty-seven Significant Natural Heritage Areas of Gaston County of national, state and regional consequence. Conducted by Dr. Alan May and funded in part by the Schiele Museum of Natural History, the report was published in 2000. Dr. May groups thirty-seven areas into three categories: Mountains & Rock Outcrops, Forests & Bogs and Stand-alone Sites. Among the items of interest are the many natural areas that contain the bigleaf magnolia tree (*Magnolia macrophylla*), which is uncommon in North Carolina. The tree was discovered and catalogued by André Michaux, who was French by birth and came to North Carolina in the late 1780s. The bigleaf magnolia has the largest simple leaf of any species in the temperate world and one of the largest flowers. The mature leaf is twenty to thirty inches long, and the blossoms are ten to fourteen inches across.

Grouped under the Mountains and Rock Outcrops category are Crowders Mountain State Park and vicinity, South Pasour Mountain, which is significant for the Piedmont Monadnock Forest, and Stagecoach Road Granitic Outcrop and Wetland. Included in the list of forests are South Crowders Creek Mesic Forest, which is a mixed hardwood forest, and North Stanley Creek Basic Forest owned by the Catawba Lands Conservancy.[3] On the border of Gaston and Lincoln Counties is the Mount Zion Heartleaf Forest, a dry-mesic, oak-hickory forest.

One of the most exciting projects planned for the Gaston County area by the Catawba Lands Conservancy is the Carolina Thread Trail project. The Carolina Thread Trail will be a unique fifteen-county project that will connect communities through a network of linked trails throughout North and South Carolina.

An Archaeological Reconnaissance of Selected Portions of Gaston County, North Carolina, printed in 1985, describes Gaston County from a geological point of view:

> Gaston County is located on the boundary between three geologic belts: inner Piedmont Belt, Kings Mountain Belt, and the Charlotte Belt. Constituents of these belts include felsic, intermediate, and mafic igneous intrusive rock, and metamorphosed intrusive volcanic and sedimentary rock. These metamorphic strata have been altered by heat and pressure to form gneisses, schists, and phylolytes. Weathering of these strata is extensive, resulting in the thick soil profiles at land surfaces. However, kyanitic quartzite resists weathering more than the above rock types and forms the higher elevations such as Crowders Mountain, Kings Mountain, Spencer Mountain, and Pasour Mountain.
>
> Strata of the inner Piedmont Belt occupy the northwest portion of the county. Constituents include layered biotite and hornblend gneisses and schists which have been intruded by 535-million-year-old Toluca granite, 350-million-year-old Cherryville granite, and an intrusive stratum of intermediate composition. To the southeast and separated by the Kings Mountain fault lays the Kings Mountain Belt which consists of volcanic and sedimentary layers. These have been metamorphosed to quart-sericite schist, hornblend, and biolite gneisses, phyllite, quartzite, and marble.[4]

Crowders Mountain State Park

Crowders Mountain, in western Gaston County, was officially designated as Crowders Mountain State Park in 1987. It includes the peaks of Crowders Mountain and Kings Pinnacle. Crowders Mountain was named for Ulrich Crowder, a German merchant and farmer who purchased the mountain and the surrounding land in 1789 before supposedly moving west. The mountain itself is an isolated mountain peak, or monadnock. The mountain rises to 1,625 feet above sea level, and the sheer rock cliffs, 100 to 150 feet in height, are a popular destination for rock climbers. Among the many trails is Crowders Trail, which is a strenuous 2.5-mile trail that winds along the base of Crowders Mountain and ultimately leads to the top. Kings Pinnacle sits at the northeast end of the Kings Mountain Range, a range of low peaks that includes Kings Mountain.[5]

Felix Walker, the first representative from Buncombe County to the United States Congress, wrote about his life in the 1760s on the Carolina frontier at Crowders Creek, stating that his father had returned from the expedition against the Cherokee, and

> purchased a beautiful tract of land on Crowder's Creek, about four miles from Kings Mountain, in the fall of 1763, being then a fresh part; he cultivated some land and raised stock...my father hunted and killed deer in abundance and maintained his family on wild meat in style. I remember he kept me following him on horse to carry the venison until I was weary of the business...He resided on Crowder's Creek until the year 1768, his ardor for range and game still continued. He purchased a tract of land for one doubloon which at this time could not be purchased for five thousand dollars; such was the value of land in half a century.

Crowders Mountain State Park rangers are seen here with visiting rangers from Burke County in the spring of 2007. *Photo by Rita Wehunt-Black.*

André Michaux and Daniel Stowe Botanical Garden

André Michaux (1746–1802), a French botanist and explorer commissioned by Louis XIV of France, arrived in New York in 1785. He bought a plantation in Charleston, South Carolina, and then spent eleven years traveling through North America collecting and identifying thousands of indigenous plants. In 1789, he discovered and named the *Magnolia macrophylla*, or bigleaf magnolia. He also discovered and named the Catawba rhododendron, which is the official flower of the Daniel Stowe Botanical Garden.

Michaux was very fond of the Carolina Piedmont, and he often followed a trail along the Catawba River. In his journal he mentioned crossing the "Tack-a-sagee" (Tuckaseege) Ford. He also walked through the site of what is today the Daniel Stowe Botanical Garden.[6]

The Daniel Stowe Botanical Garden is located at 6500 South New Hope Road near Belmont. Daniel J. Stowe[7] descends from Abraham Stowe Sr., who was born in 1762 in Virginia and, along with his two brothers, came to the Gaston County area in 1810.

CHAPTER 2

The Scots-Irish and the Carolina Backcountry

The Scottish migration to America involved several groups. First there were the Lowland Scots, who sought opportunity in America. Then there were the Highlanders, who were somewhat clannish. Every summer Grandfather Mountain, near Linville, North Carolina, is host to the largest gathering of clans in the United States.

The Scots-Irish (who were not Irish at all, though some intermarrying with the Irish did occur) composed the majority of the Scots who came to America. The Scots-Irish were actually Scottish Lowlanders who moved to Northern Ireland in the seventeenth century. They were the largest group of immigrants arriving in America in the eighteenth century. It is estimated that nine out of ten Scots-Irish had to become indentured servants to pay for their passage, but being indentured did not necessarily mean that they were uneducated.

The Scots-Irish were a restless people who carried their migratory ways from Britain to America. Their history was a series of removals. They had moved from Scotland to Ireland, from Ireland to Pennsylvania, from Pennsylvania to the Carolinas and, in some cases, farther south and west.[8] The early Scots-Irish settled in New York, New Jersey and Pennsylvania. After 1730, many moved into Virginia and the backcountry of the Carolinas. By the eve of the American Revolution more than a million Scots-Irish immigrants had come to the American colonies in less than fifty years.

These Scots-Irish Presbyterians left Pennsylvania, Maryland and Virginia and traveled down the Great Wagon Road through the Shenandoah Valley starting in the 1740s and '50s. They would be the first permanent settlers west of the Catawba River. Some stayed over in Virginia for a year or two with other Scots-Irish settlers and then continued on to the Catawba River.

Charles Woodmason, an English Anglican minister, was sent into the backcountry of the Carolinas when the Anglican Church, the official church of the colony, began taking notice of the ever-increasing population of Presbyterians in the backcountry. In order to try to convert some of "these heathens" to the "correct religion," a number of ministers were sent. Charles Woodmason had some very scathing comments about the residents of the region. His disgust was reserved primarily for the Presbyterians, whom he referred to as those "ignorant, mean, worthless, beggarly Irish Presbyterians, the Scum of the Earth, and Refuse of Mankind." Woodmason also had rather derogatory comments for Quakers, Catholics and Baptists:

> *Not less than 20 itinerant Presbyterian, Baptist and Independent Preachers are maintain'd by the Synods of Pennsylvania and New England to traverse this Country Poisoning the Minds of the People—Instilling Democratical and Commonwealth Principles into their minds.— Embittering them against the very name of Bishops, and all Episcopal Government and laying deep their fatal Republican Notions and Principles—Especially that they owe no Subjection to Great Britain—They are a free people—That they are to pay allegiance to King George as their Sovereign—But as to Great Britain or the Parliament, or any there, that they have no more to think of or about them than the Turk or Pope—Thus do these Itinerant Preachers sent from the Northern Colonies pervert the Minds of the Vulgar.*

The Land Between the Rivers

The Catawba River begins in springs in the Black Mountains, about ten miles below Mount Mitchell. After many small falls, not far from Marion, it is joined by the Linville River. This river is full of rocky shoals. The South Fork River is formed by the confluence of the Henry River and Jacob's River in southwestern Catawba County. The South Fork's main tributary is Clark's Creek, which empties into the South Fork near Lincolnton. The South Fork River splits Gaston and Lincoln Counties as it flows south into the Catawba River.

John Lawson, an English naturalist, was commissioned by the Lords Proprietors, the royal governors of the Carolinas, to make a (reconnaissance) survey of the interior. Lawson's party traveled from Charles Town up the Santee-Wateree River Basin and crude trails. In the winter of 1701, they "came upon the place where two broad rivers rushed together."[9] The two rivers Lawson saw rushing together were the Catawba River and the South Fork River.[10] Lawson and his men must have looked across that confluence at a point where the forests rose and spread northwest. The peninsula would become known as "the Point."[11] The people who Lawson saw would become known as the Catawba Indians. They called themselves *Nieye* or "real people." The Catawba Indians believed their namesake river offered food, trade and spirituality.[12]

When the Scots-Irish began moving southward and drifting west of the Catawba River into the area that would become eastern Gaston County, they settled mostly along the banks of the Catawba and South Fork Rivers. These Scots-Irish were of Presbyterian faith. Prior to the American Revolution, of the thirty-four earliest churches found in an eighteen-county region of the Carolina Piedmont stretching from Rowan County, North Carolina, to Fairfield County, South Carolina, thirty-one of them were Presbyterian.[13]

The Scots-Irish settlements and their meetinghouses, as well as the homes of their ministers and leaders, became rallying points for those of like sentiments. Most of the Scots-Irish, whether through direct dealings or by way of family traditions, continued to harbor great resentments toward the Crown even after their settlement, and this in turn brought to the backcountry a ready-made group of "born rebels," as one British officer called them in 1778. An unknown Hessian officer, recording his observations on the Revolutionary War, wrote, "Call this war by whatever name you may, only call it not an American Rebellion: it is nothing more or less than a Scotch-Irish Presbyterian Rebellion."

Minnie Stowe Puett (1871–1945), in her 1939 book *History of Gaston County*, had this to say about the first recorded settlers to the Point around 1750:

> *...the Point, so called from the neck of land jutting out into the water at the confluence of the South Fork and Catawba Rivers. Among those settling there were Frederick Hambright, German; the Hardins, Hambright's brothers-in-law, English; Robert Leeper, English; James Kuykendall, Dutch, who later settled on Dutchman's Creek which was named for him; Alexander McLean, Scotch-Irish; and doubtless many others...The records show that the Scotch-Irish were a thrifty people of whom it is said that "they keep the Sabbath and everything else they get their hands on"...they were shrewd enough to enter large tracts of land or, as is often recorded, several tracts in different sections of a territory. Then, as the old deeds show, they sold to other pioneers who came in.*

Thomas Robertson was issued a grant dated April 13, 1749. Robert Leeper was also one of the first known settlers near the Point. His earliest land grant for 350 acres was issued March 31, 1750. James Kuykendall's first recorded grant for 600 acres was entered September 28, 1750.[14]

As protection against Catawba and Cherokee raids, Kuykendall, Leeper and others built a log fort and stockade at the junction of the South Fork and Catawba Rivers at the foot of a bluff.[15] The building was within a triangular enclosure, formed by a stockade on one side that began at the Catawba River and ended at a point on the South Fork River, with the rivers forming the other two sides.[16]

Others holding early grants in the area were: Robert Palmer, Robert Patterson, Robert Patrick, William Patten, Rachel Price, Robert Ramsey, George Penick, James Sharpe, David Templeton, John Thomas, John Turner, William Barnett and Edward Boyle.[17] On the lower South Fork, John Armstrong obtained a grant dated August 30, 1753, for 350 acres on the Belmont side of Armstrong's Ford; and Major Chronicle purchased from William Barnett the land on which he lived and on which the town of Belmont is now located.[18]

Goshen Presbyterian Church

Almost 250 years ago Goshen Presbyterian Church was formed. It was Gaston County's first Presbyterian Church and probably the first Presbyterian Church west of the Catawba River in North Carolina. Its first formal organization was by Scots-Irish Presbyterians in 1764; but, as was often the case in those early days, a graveyard was started and then a church was built near the graveyard. The church was located just north of what is today Belmont.

The first person to be buried in what is called the Old Goshen Graveyard was a traveler who had been passing through the area searching for a place to settle. He was camped near a spring by a grove of trees where all-day preaching was often held. He fell ill and was nursed by the women of the settlement. When he died, he was buried on a hill above the camp; and later others from the settlement were buried near the stranger. Soon a brush arbor was built near the graveyard, and it was later replaced by a log church. In time, a larger log church was built on the opposite hill, and in 1839 a frame church building replaced it.

The formal organization that took place in 1764 was led by Reverends Elisha Spencer and Alexander McWorter, who were acting as a commission from the Synod of New York and Philadelphia and were sent "to the back parts of North Carolina for the express purpose of organization of churches and assisting them in settling their boundaries." In 1767 there is a record in the minutes of the Synod of New York and Philadelphia that states, "Goshen in the forks of the Catawba, petitions for someone to preach for them."

In 1793 Goshen Church extended a call to Dr. Humphrey Hunter for half of his time. Some of the prominent men of the congregation signed the call and guaranteed an annual salary of sixty-two pounds, ten shillings.

The following known Revolutionary War Patriots are buried at Goshen Cemetery: Robert Alexander, Hugh Berry, Andrew Berry, Richard Berry, Samuel Caldwell, Thomas Campbell, George Cathey, Hugh Ewing, Peter Fite, John Gleen, James Gullick, Thomas Hanks, Thomas Henry, Samuel Martin, Alexander Moore, John Moore, George Oliver, William Rankin, Samuel Rankin, James Rutledge, Abraham Scott and John Smith.

Goshen, like many other early churches, depended on itinerant and "missionary" preachers who came anywhere from two to four times a year. The coming of a preacher was an exciting time. Men and women traveled on foot and horseback from miles around to the

Goshen Cemetery on Woodlawn Road in North Belmont was established in 1764. Many Revolutionary War soldiers are buried here. Goshen Presbyterian Church, built around 1760, once stood nearby. *Photo by Rita Wehunt-Black.*

church. The ministers, along with the sacraments, brought letters and news from those left behind in Pennsylvania and Virginia.

The 1800s were a time of growth for Goshen Church. We get a brief picture of life in the 1800s at Goshen from Session Records and other documents from that time. In 1882, in his notes, Dr. R.Z. Johnson, who lived in Lincolnton, North Carolina, and usually went to Goshen by horse or cart, wrote that "Goshen congregation sent about 30 bushels of wheat, some flour, oats, chickens, and vegetables in two wagons to the pastor during the year."

In the 1856 will of Andrew Hoyle (1771–1857) of Dallas, we find his wishes, "I will that my executors shall pay to the churches at Goshen and Dallas 15 dollars per annum to each church for 6 years as stipend for the ministry at those places, providing that they are Presbyterian."

Goshen eventually outgrew the frame church of 1839, and at a later point Goshen Church was moved to a site near the Stowe Spinning community in North Belmont.

Many of the county's early settlers, cotton mill founders, ministers and educators were at one time on the rolls of Goshen Church. Some of the early Scots-Irish families were: Love, Martin, Rutledge, Rankin, Moore, Johnson, Alexander, Johnston, Johnson, Smith, Caldwell, Dickson, Boyd, Hall, Hunter, Roach, Abernethy, Hutchison, Sparrow, Ratchford and Miller.

The following Presbyterian Churches grew out of Goshen: New Hope Presbyterian, Dallas Presbyterian, Belmont Presbyterian, Mount Holly Presbyterian, Stanley Presbyterian, Castanea Presbyterian and, indirectly, Lowell Presbyterian and East Belmont Presbyterian.

Olney Presbyterian Church

Olney Presbyterian Church in Gastonia was formed from Bethel Presbyterian Church in York County, South Carolina, and its history intertwines with the Scots-Irish immigration from Pennsylvania to the Carolinas and Old Tryon County, North Carolina.

No records exist, but tradition says that Olney Presbyterian Church was formed as a separate church from Bethel in 1793; some say even earlier. The state line between North and South Carolina is said to have been the dividing line between the two congregations.

In April 1827 Olney reported to Bethel Presbytery forty-four members. Official records for Olney start in 1839. In 1864 a wood-frame church was built, and then in 1930 the present-day brick church was constructed.

In 1882 fifty-two members left Olney and formed a new church in Gastonia called First Presbyterian Church of Gastonia. Joining the regular membership in this new church were some of Olney's church officials, including Captain J.Q Holland, R.C.G. Love, James R. Shannon, Robert Bell and Dr. R.H. Adams.

The beautiful Olney Cemetery, with one section originally a slave cemetery, is quite large. The oldest grave has a date of 1795. There are many Revolutionary War Patriots buried in Olney Churchyard: Adam Baird, Robert Baird, John Berry, Elisha Cox, William Gregory, Isaac Holland, John Kincaid, John Martin, John Massey, Nathan Mendenhall, John Moore, Thomas Price, William Price, Alexander Robinson, James Robinson, John Wilson and James Witherspoon. There may be others.

Olney Presbyterian Church in Gastonia was organized in 1793, and the oldest grave has a date of 1795. Seventeen known Revolutionary War Patriots are buried in the churchyard. One section was originally a slave cemetery. *Photo by Rita Wehunt-Black.*

Eventually, five textile mills were built within sight of the church and hundreds of people came to live in the mill villages that surrounded the mills. By 1940 the Presbytery showed a total of 294 members.

No one in Gaston County should miss seeing this church and cemetery. In this churchyard one can indeed feel the connection to Gaston County's past.

CHAPTER 3

Pathfinders, Pioneers
and Patriots

Tryon County Court was organized at Charles McLean's home, and the quarter sessions for the years 1769, 1770 and 1771 were held there. He lived in the southern part of what is now Gaston County, on the headwaters of Crowders Creek, near Crowders Mountain. Court dates for 1773 and 1774 were held at Christopher Carpenter's home in the Beaverdam Settlement.

On July 26, 1774, residents selected the place on which the courthouse, prison and stocks for Tryon County would be built. The place selected was "the crossroads on Christopher Mauney's land, between the heads of Long Creek, Muddy Creek and Beaver Dam Creek in the county before said as most central and convenient for the purpose aforesaid." The county court was to meet at the "house of Christy Mauney or the crossroads in his land." The Tryon Court House site sits on North Carolina Highway 274, near the intersection with Tryon School Road, in Cherryville Township. The October 1774 Sessions were held at the house of Christian Mauney, and a room in his dwelling was used as a jail.

Alfred Nixon, in his 1910 *The History of Lincoln County*, describes Old Tryon County:

> with its fine farms and beautiful homes, dotted with towns and villages, and musical with the hum of machinery, the pioneers found a wild, luxuriant with native flora, the habitat of the red man and wild animals. There were herds of fleet-footed deer; there were clumsy brown bear and fierce wild cats and panthers; there were droves of buffalo, and countless beavers building their dams on the creeks. The early settlers waged a relentless war on these animals and set a bounty on many of their scalps. The scalps on which a price was set were the wolf, panther, wild cat, and such other as preyed on domestic animals. For killing a grown wolf the price was one pound; a young wolf ten shillings; a wild cat five shillings... We still retain Indian, Beaver Dam, and Buffalo Creeks, Bear Ford, Wolf Gulch, and Buffalo Mountain, Buffalo Shoals, and the Indian names Catawba and Tuckaseegee, memorials to these primeval days.

It was in the above setting that Christian Mauney's home was said to sit, at a crossroads. One road led to the Beatty's Ford over the Catawba River and the other to the Tuckaseegee

The state marker at the site of Tryon County Court House (1774–1783), located in the Tryon Community in western Gaston County. Tryon County was named for the colonial governor, William Tryon. *Photo by Rita Wehunt-Black.*

Ford. An archaeological reconnaissance of the (Christian) Mauney Family Association Tract was done in 2004, and the findings were published by Tracy Martin, John D. Bolick, Darlene Philyaw, Jerod Shuford and J. Alan May, PhD. Their findings stated,

> *Though we cannot, through archaeological evidence, state the exact location of the Christian Mauney home, we can say, with certainty, that there is a high probability it was somewhere on or near the tract currently owned by the Mauney Family Association. Based on the available information we conclude that it is likely that the Christian Mauney house was located on the site where the modern Tryonota Fire Department now stands, as there is strong evidence to support this idea.*[19]

Christian Mauney and his family were very busy during this time. In the Tryon County Court records it is noted that Christian Mauney was the caretaker of the section of the road

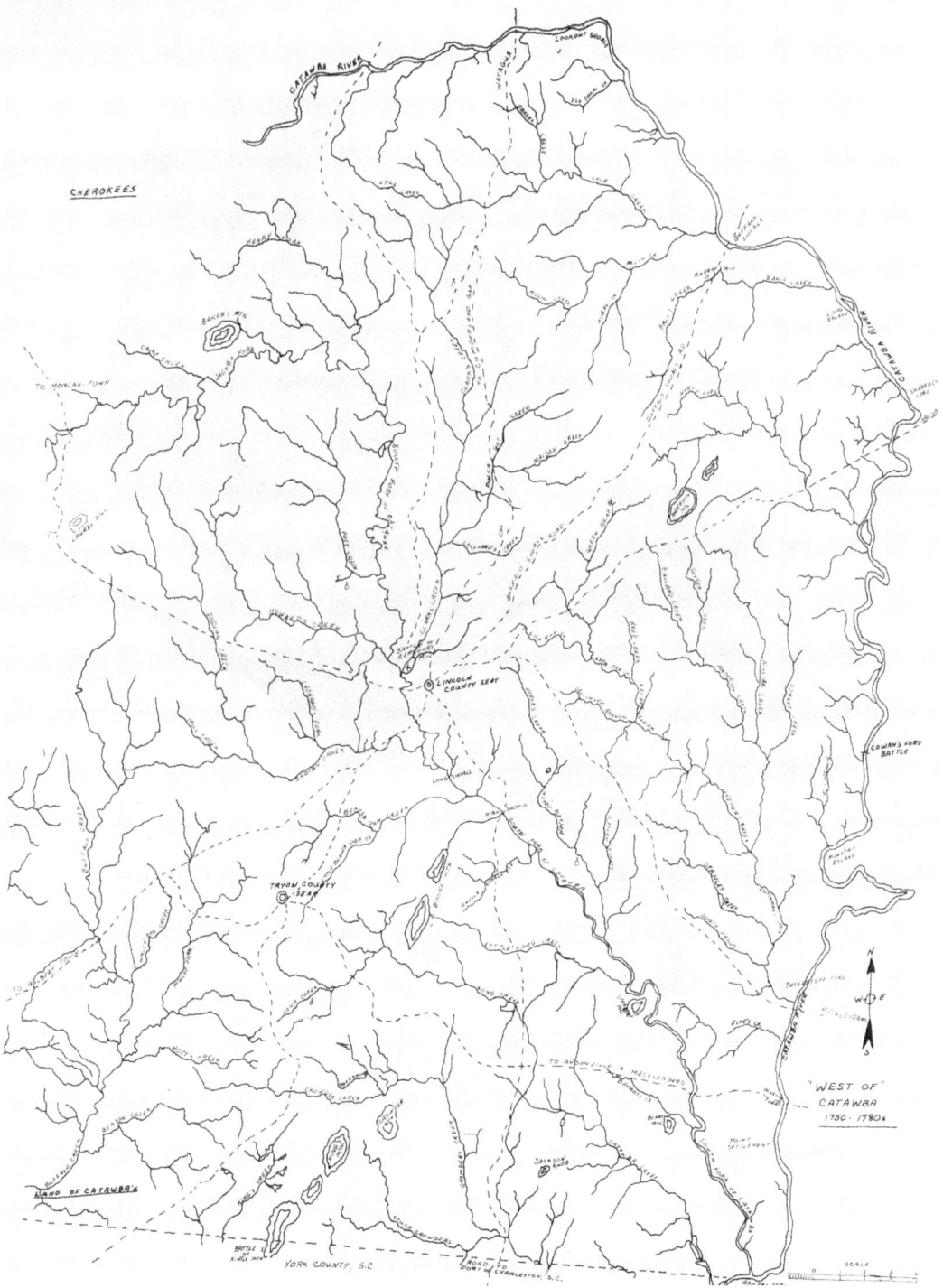

West of the Catawba River, 1750–1780. *Map courtesy of Rita Wehunt-Black*

that ran on his property. He would also ask for a permit to open an ordinary in October of 1774. In the 1700s, public drinking establishments went by a variety of names. They were called ordinaries, inns, taverns, dramshops, groggeries, public houses or alehouses and were plentiful on the Great Wagon Road that ran from Pennsylvania to the Carolinas. Very few records of these establishments exist today. Daniel B. Thorp, in *The Southern Colonial Backcountry*, tells us,

> *a tavern is any establishment that regularly offered alcohol, meals, and/or lodging to the public for a fee…Between 1753 and 1776, the Rowan County Court used all three terms (taverns, ordinaries and public houses) to describe what it was licensing.*

A lot of tavern keepers never obtained a license. Thorp's analysis of the existing tavern records for Rowan County, North Carolina, in the 1770s allows us to identify ethnic enclaves within the mixed ethnicity of its immigrant population of English, German and Scots-Irish. Thorp sums up some of these findings for what was then Rowan County:

> *Throughout Rowan County, distilled spirits—whiskey, rum, and brandy—were served more often than beer, but the ratio of spirits to beer varied from place to place. The more Scottish a tavern's clientele, the more spirits it served. In the Lowrances' ledger, 71 percent of the ethnically distinctive surnames were Scottish, while English and German names, together, made up just 12.5 percent…The mainstay of their* [The Lowrances' Tavern] *trade identified usually as "liquor" in their account book, was a form of whiskey made from corn and rye, although they also sold significant amounts of (peach) brandy…rum brought from Charles Town: and a few months in 1767, a batch of locally produced mathiglein, a type of mead. William Steele, on the other hand, sold a much greater variety of drinks and fewer local products. From merchants in Charles Town he purchased two kinds of rum, plus Madeira, claret and another unnamed wine.*[20]

In the "Tryon County Court Minutes," July Court 1770, the rates to be charged in ordinaries were set as follows:

	Pound
Lodging in a Good feather Bed & Clean Sheets P'r Night	*.004*
Breakfast & Supper Each	*.008*
Every dinner not Less than 2 dishes of Good Meat	*.010*
Madeira & Port wine P'r Quart	*.030*
Claret wine P'r Quart	*.040*
Punch with Loaf Sugar & West India Rum P'r Qu't	*.016*
Toddy with Loaf Sugar & West India Rum P'r Quart	*.014*
Toddy with Loaf Sugar & English Rum P'r Quart	*.008*
Brandy & Whisky Toddy P'r ½ pint	*.004*
Beer P'r Quart	*.006*
Cider P'r Quarter	*.006*
W. India Rum P'r ½ pint	*.010*

New England Rum P'r ½ pint	*.006*
Brandy or Whisky P'r ½ pint	*.006*
Pasturage for every horse or mare for 24 hours	*.004*
Stabling for Every night w't hay or fodder for Every Horse or Mare	*.010*[21]

Of all inns and taverns in the colonies, those operated by Germans were generally considered the best. The Germanic respect for cleanliness and good food showed up in such establishments.[22]

The following is part of an article that was printed in the *Cherryville Eagle* on September 25, 1919, about the unveiling of the monument at the Mauney homestead site:

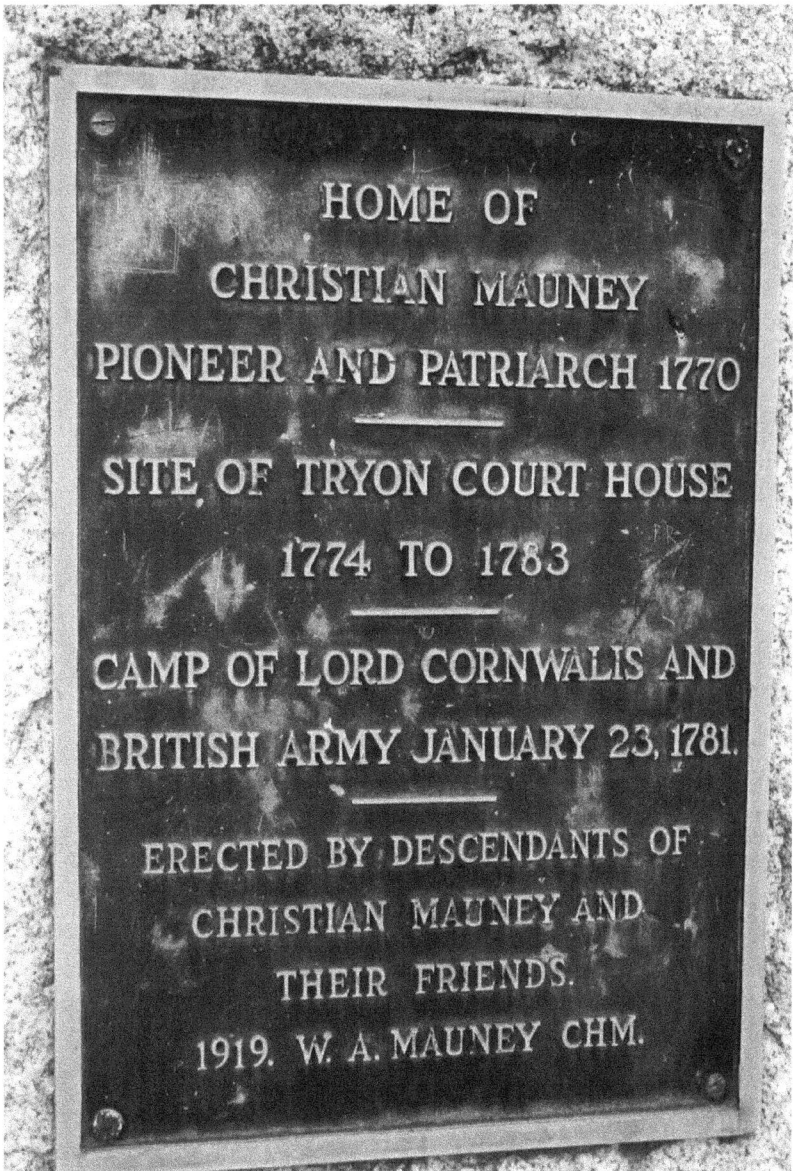

Erected by descendents of Christian Mauney and friends in 1919, this monument marks the site of Christian Mauney's home and Tryon County Court House (1774–1783). *Photo by Rita Wehunt-Black.*

The fourth annual reunion of the descendants of Christian Mauney was held last Saturday at the old homestead of Christian Mauney, four miles south of Cherryville on the Bessemer City Road. The courts of old Tryon County were held at this old homestead for nine years during his residence at this historic spot.

A large number of descendants of this old pioneer and their friends attended the reunion. The principal speaker for the occasion was Lieut. Gov. O. Max Gardner, who was introduced by Hon. W.A. Mauney, chairman of the Mauney Memorial Association. At the conclusion of Mr. Gardner's very interesting address replete with historic facts associated with this place… the monument was unveiled by Misses Virginia Mauney and Pru Hagar…The Mauney Memorial Association has recently purchased four acres of land on which the monument stands, also including the site of the Old Christian Mauney residence.

Regulators, Tories and the Formation of a County

Among the earliest settlers of the Catawba Valley was the Moore family. Linda Moore Bollinger, in her wonderfully documented book *The Leading Edge, A History of the Family of Aaron Moore, Pennsylvania Indian Trader & North Carolina Pioneer*, follows the lives of her Moore ancestors as they settled in the Carolinas in the 1750s and struggled with the decision between Whig or Tory, Patriot or Loyalist. Their choices would divide the family and affect their lives and the lives of others long, long after the American Revolution had ended.

Following the Moore family, or any family who settled very early to the west of the Catawba River in what is now Gaston County, also traces the formation of Gaston County as it morphed from Bladen County into Anson County, then into Mecklenburg, Tryon and Lincoln Counties and finally into Gaston County.

At the time the Moore family arrived, the South Fork of the Catawba River was in Old Anson County; Anson having been formed from the western part of Bladen in 1748. The area had few settlers, and the first mention of the Moore family in the Old Anson County records states,

On 13 & 14 August 1755, Moses Moore purchased from Richard Renelds [Reynolds] land on the south side of south fork cuttawba [Catawba], on Renols [Reynolds] Creek, including where he lately lived, 600 A [acres] granted to Renelds 28 March 1755.[23]

The section of Reynolds Creek, also known as Indian Creek, was located near present-day Cherryville. Less than two months later, on October 25, 1755, John Moore bought six hundred acres on Indian Creek from Evan and Mary Lewis.[24] Moore's land was very close to his brother Moses's land and may have even joined that of his brother. On October 21, 1758, Aaron Moore was granted a "Crown" patent for two hundred acres in Anson County on both sides of Indian Creek, including his own improvements.

Aaron Moore's brother, John Moore, soon attained the rank of captain in the North Carolina Colonial Militia. In the *Colonial Records of North Carolina*[25] there is a letter to General Hugh Waddell, Mr. Osburn and Mr. Alexander from Governor Arthur Dobbs, New Bern, dated July 18, 1756:

I am sorry to find…by the two petitions deliver'd to me by Captains Green and Moore from the settlers on the Broad River and South Catauba [Catawba] River that there has been several abuses and robberies committed by strolling parties of Indians who…have reason to believe… are Cherokee Indians headed by some Fr. Indians and perhaps two or three Northern Indians the French have brought with them…upon the petitions sent to me and to put an end to the fears of the inhabitants I have given to Captain Green and Moor[e] each a commission to command a scout to patrol whilst necessary but to be under your command to be called in as soon as you find it safe and prudent…I have also told Messrs. Green and Moore that if they will make any fort at their own expense to protect themselves I will recommend them to the Assembly to be reimbust [reimbursed] as far as their expense comes to…

On October 5, 1756, "His Excellency the Governor" sent two petitions to the House, one from the frontier inhabitants of Broad River and the other from the inhabitants of the South Fork of the Catawba River, setting forth the great hardships they endured and the damages that had been done to them and their hogs, goods and chattels by several "Indians."[26]

Concerned for the safety of the frontier, officials in North Carolina organized a company of rangers in 1756 to patrol the backcountry and help settlers defend themselves against Native American attacks. Hugh Waddell was given command and was partly responsible for negotiating a treaty that kept the Catawba and Cherokee on the side of the British in the French and Indian War (1754–1763). Several forts were built around this time, including Fort Dobbs near present-day Statesville.

The Native American attacks continued in the Catawba Valley. Some settlers were forced to leave their homes, and some settlers were killed. After the Native Americans attempted unsuccessfully to attack Fort Dobbs, an expedition under Colonel Archibald Montgomery, consisting of sixteen hundred Scottish Highlanders and colonists, was organized to do battle with the Cherokee. More than fifteen Native American villages were destroyed, and the expedition went as far as the town of Franklin. The Cherokee, who had been previously warned, waited for Montgomery's men in ambush at Echoee on June 27, 1760.

Future expeditions into the Cherokee's land eventually pushed the Cherokee Indians back and broke their power to prevent the takeover of their land. A joint campaign with Virginia against the Cherokee had resulted in the Cherokee signing a peace treaty in December 1761. This ended fighting along the Carolina frontier, although the Treaty of Paris that officially ended the war was not signed until February 1763.

In 1763, Mecklenburg was formed from Anson County and the South Fork of the Catawba River lay in the new county of Mecklenburg. Around this time, Moses Moore replaced his brother John as captain in the local militia. Also around this time there was another Moore family, headed by Guyan Moore, living on Leonard's Fork of Indian Creek.[27]

More and more settlers took up the unclaimed land along the South Fork River. In 1765 Aaron Moore was a chain bearer when Frances Beatey added to his holdings on Indian Creek. John Walker, from New Castle, Delaware, arrived at the foot of Crowders Mountain in 1763.[28]

Some of the Moores were resettling near the Broad River and Second Broad River now that the Cherokee were not a problem. Aaron Moore moved to the Second Broad River in 1768. In that year, Aaron Moore and his wife Rachel sold to Peter Carpenter two hundred acres on both sides of Indian Creek that had been granted to Moore on October 23, 1758.[29]

In 1768, another new county was formed. The South Fork and all the land to the west, including the Second Broad River, lay in the new county. The new county was to be called Tryon, named for Governor William Tryon of the Province of North Carolina. Tryon was a hated man, with his palace at New Bern, and bitterness brewed.

From the Tryon County Court records we can see that Aaron Moore was a respected man in the new county, and he was frequently called to serve as a member of the grand jury. In the late 1700s in North Carolina, each county was divided into taxing districts and the head of each district was called a captain, elected by the men of his company. By 1775, Aaron Moore held the rank of captain.

After years of unrest among backcountry settlers and the regulators, Royal Governor William Tryon led the colonial militia from Eastern North Carolina to victory at the Battle of Alamance on May 16, 1771. This was known as the War of Regulation, the last of the major colonial conflicts and a prelude to the American Revolution in North Carolina.

Aaron, his brother Moses Moore and their friend John Walker were among the first associated with revolutionary ideas in the area.[30] Settlers, not knowing how a conflict between the colonies and England would turn out, tended at first not to take sides. But, despite lack of popular support, Tryon County was becoming a Tory stronghold, and those discontented with British rule continued their subversive political activities.

In July of 1775, the freeholders of Tryon County chose five delegates to attend a convention in Hillsboro in August of 1775. The purpose was to protest the British government's certain grievances of the North Carolina colonists. One of the delegates chosen was John Walker. On July 26, the freeholders of Tryon County met to organize a safety committee. Three members were elected from each company; from Captain Aaron Moore's company were John Walker, John Beaman and George Black.[31]

On August 14, 1775, the members of this safety committee met at Christian Mauney's house and passed resolutions, including the following, signed by twenty-three members of the safety committee and twenty-six freeholders. The "Tryon Declaration of Independence" or Tryon Resolve reads as follows:

> *The unprecedented, barbarous and bloody actions committed by the British Troops on our American Brethren near Boston on the 19th of April and 20th of May last, together with the Hostile Operations and Traiterous Designs now carrying on by the Tools of Ministerial Vengeance and Despotism for the Subjugating all British America, suggest to us the painful necessity of having recourse to Arms for the preservation of those Rights and Liberties which the principles of our Constitution and the Laws of God, Nature and Nations have made it our duty to defend.*
>
> *We, therefore, the Subscribers, Freeholders and Inhabitants of Tryon County, do hereby faithfully unite ourselves under the most sacred ties of Religion, Honor and Love to our Country, firmly to resist force by force in defense of our National Freedom and Constitutional Rights against all invasions, and at the same time do solemnly engage to take up Arms*

and Risque our lives and fortunes in maintaining the freedom of our Country, whenever the Wisdom and Council of the Continental Congress or our Provincial Convention shall declare it necessary, and this Engagement we will continue in and hold sacred til a Reconciliation shall take place between Great Britain and America on Constitutional principles which we most ardently desire. And we do firmly agree to hold all such persons Inimical to the liberties of America, who shall refuse to subscribe to this Association.

The document was signed by John Walker, Charles McLean, Andrew Neel, Thomas Beatty, James Corburn, Frederick Hambright, Andrew Hampton, Benjamin Hardin, George Paris, William Graham, Robt. Alexander, David Jenkins, Thomas Espey, James McAfee, William Thompson, Samuel Carpenter, Richard Woffer, Jacob Forney, David Whitesides, John Beaman, John Morris, Joseph Harden, John Robison, Valentine Mauney, George Black, James Logan, Jas. Baird, Christian Carpenter, Abel Beatty, Joab Turner, Jonathan Price, Jam. Miller, John Dellinger, James McIntire, Jacob Mauney Jr., John Wells, Jacob Costner, Robert Hulclip, James Buchanan, Moses Moore, Joseph Kuykendall, Adam Simms, Samuel Smith, Joseph Neel, Samuel Loftin and Peregrine Mackness.

This document was located years later in the papers of General William Graham and today is located in the North Carolina State Archives in Raleigh.

Revolutionary War

In 1777, it was ordered that all men of age sign an oath of allegiance. The penalty for failure to sign was confiscation of property and banishment. Almost everyone in Tryon County signed the oath, even Tory sympathizers.[32]

John Moore, son of Moses was named as a Tory in an Act of Assembly in 1779. He led a party of Tories from Tryon County to Georgia in early February where he united with Colonel Boyd.[33] McLean and his followers drove out several families with "unacceptable politics," but they did not find John Moore. He had escaped Kettle Creek and in December of 1779 was observed near Mosley's Ferry on "the Ogeechee."

Charleston fell to the British on May 12, 1780, and on June 7, 1780, Lieutenant Colonel John Moore, a member of John Hamilton's Corps of North Carolina Loyalists, galloped up to his father's house on Indian Creek to tell him the news of the fall of Charleston. He had a fine horse, wore a fine uniform trimmed in gold braid and carried a sword. Sources differ on whether his men were in tatters or glitteringly impressive. Colonel Moore had orders to muster as many local Tories as he could.[34]

On June 10, 1780, Colonel Moore and Tories from Lincoln and Rutherford Counties were excited about the fall of Charleston, and Moore summoned his men, with a few Hessians among them, to muster near Indian Creek. There they were told to go home, harvest their crops and store them for the arrival of Cornwallis's army in the fall.

When the news came that Major Joseph McDowell and about twenty Whigs were nearby, the Tories decided to attack McDowell, but he had already retreated to the mountains near the Lincoln and Burke County line, today called the South Mountains. The next day Moore set up a Tory camp on a tributary of Indian Creek, known as Camp Branch, about a half mile from his father's home. On the thirteenth and fourteenth he was joined by Major Welch and a large number of Loyalists.[35]

After an unsuccessful five-day attempt to capture Colonel Hugh Brevard, Major McDowell and the Whigs, Moore gathered nearly thirteen hundred Tories on June 20 below Ramseur's Mill. As word of the Tory camp reached Whig General Rutherford, he gave orders to Colonel Frances Locke of Rowan County and Major McDowell to disperse the Tory army.

The Whig militia combed throughout the area in search of Moore. They went to the home of Moses Moore, John Moore's father, several times. According to various Revolutionary War pension records, Moses Moore was harassed by the Whigs several times. One such Revolutionary War pension record belonging to Robert Knox, read in part,

> *Robert Knox served under Colonel McLean in pursuit of Col. John Moore in command of a party of Tories. They* [the Whigs] *marched to Moses Moore's, father of the colonel, and started to destroy his oats by turning their horses into the crop, but the officers came up and prevented it.*

On June 19, 1780, Colonel Moore moved his troop of thirteen hundred Loyalists to Ramseur's Mill, located near Lincolnton, where they camped on a ridge for the night.

The battle that came the next day was tragic for Colonel Moore. Due to a surprise attack by Colonel Locke, who had been informed of Moore's position by Whig Adam Reep, John Moore did not realize that his men outnumbered the approximately four hundred Whig Soldiers. After the battle, more than seventy men lay dead on the battlefield, a hundred were wounded and fifty Tories had been captured.

Colonel Moore decided against a counterattack when he heard that General Rutherford and a thousand men were on their way to help the other Whigs. Colonel Moore, with about thirty of his followers, escaped and fled to the British at Camden, South Carolina, where Moore was threatened with a court-martial for having led the Loyalists into action before the appointed time.

On October 7, 1780, American Patriots destroyed Ferguson's forces at the Battle of Kings Mountain. At the time of this battle, Colonel John Moore and his men were off on a foraging expedition and had escaped Kings Mountain.

On April 11, 1783, London's *Political Magazine* published the statement of a North Carolina Loyalist who claimed that Colonel John Moore had been taken prisoner by Colonel Wade Hampton near the Wateree River and hanged.[36] Family tradition, passed from John Moore's sister to her grandson John H. Roberts, states that John Moore went to his father's birthplace at Carlisle, England, and was lost track of there. Moses Moore, John Moore's father, left Lincoln County after the war and moved to West Florida (at that time possessed by the Spanish).[37]

A Revolutionary War reenactment at the Howser House, located in a remote part of the Kings Mountain National Military Park. The stone structure was built by Henry Howser in 1803. *Photo by Rita Wehunt-Black.*

The Overmountain Men's Victory Trail

In September of 1780 a military campaign began that ended in the American victory at the Battle of Kings Mountain. Historians now agree that the battle by Patriot frontier militiamen was a turning point in the Revolutionary War.

On September 12, 1780, Burke County militiamen under the command of Charles McDowell skirmished with a part of British Major Patrick Ferguson's Loyalist army at Cane Creek and then retreated over the Appalachian Mountains to Sycamore Shoals (present-day Elizabethtown, Tennessee).

Patriot militiaman Samuel Phillips, a prisoner of war, after being released by Ferguson quickly delivered a threatening message from Ferguson to Isaac Shelby in the Overmountain regions of North Carolina. Shelby rode forty miles to the home of John Sevier. Shelby and

Sevier talked about the threat and agreed to send messengers to call for a muster of militia at Sycamore Shoals.

Hearing the call, Colonel William Campbell left from Craig's Meadow (today Abingdon, Virginia) on September 24 with 200 Virginia militiamen. Colonel Arthur Campbell rode out along the Watauga Road with another group of 200 men. The next day 480 militiamen from the Overmountain regions of North Carolina (today Tennessee) mustered at Sycamore Shoals with the militiamen from Virginia and 160 militiamen from Burke County, North Carolina.

On September 26 the Overmountain Men rode toward the mountains driving a herd of cattle to feed the army; they camped at Shelving Rock, beneath which they stored their powder to keep it dry. They crossed the Roan Mountain through the Yellow Mountain Gap not knowing exactly what dangers lay beyond. They arrived at the crest of the mountain in snow "shoe mouth deep." It was there that they discovered that two men known to have Tory leanings were missing. They had deserted to warn Ferguson of the approaching army of Patriots.

Meanwhile, in the northern part of the Piedmont of North Carolina, 350 Wilkes-Surry County Patriots, led by Major Joseph Winston and Colonel Benjamin Cleveland, rode upstream along the Yadkin River toward Quaker Meadows. The Overmountain Men moved along the North Toe River and camped near present-day Spruce Pine, North Carolina.

On September 29 the Patriots divided into two groups near Gillespie Gap and descended the Blue Ridge Mountains following separate routes. They camped at Turkey Cove and North Cove. The next day the two groups rode along separate routes near the Catawba River and reunited along the way. They camped at Quaker Meadows where they were joined by the Wilkes-Surry militia and others. Seeing such a large group lifted the spirits of the men.

The combined army of over fourteen hundred men headed south toward Gilbert Town (present-day Rutherfordton, North Carolina) where they expected to find Ferguson's army. In the late afternoon the Patriots stopped at Bedford Hill in South Mountain Gap because of heavy rain. Continuing rain kept the men in camp all day October 2. While they were camped, the leaders met and elected William Campbell as their commander.

On October 3 the militiamen prepared for battle and moved toward Gilbert Town along Cane Creek. They didn't pitch tent; the men slept the best way they could.

On October 4 the Patriots arrived at Gilbert Town, but found Ferguson gone. They sent out scouts to learn if Ferguson was heading for the fort at Ninety-Six (in South Carolina) or heading for Charlotte, and then they continued south. The next day the Patriots headed southwest and camped at Alexander's Ford on the Green River. They learned from their scouts that Ferguson was heading toward Charlotte and the protection of Cornwallis's army.

On October 6 the Patriots rode southeast toward Cowpens where they were joined by militiamen from South Carolina, Georgia and Lincoln County, North Carolina (present-day Gaston and Lincoln Counties). They learned that Ferguson was only thirty-five miles away, camped at Kings Mountain. Nine hundred of the best marksmen were chosen, along with nine hundred of the fastest horses. At 9:00 p.m. these Patriots rode off into the night. The cold rain continued.

On the night of October 7 the Patriots rode all night, forded the rain-swollen Broad River and encircled Kings Mountain at 3:00 p.m. the following day.

In one hour the Patriots killed or captured Ferguson's entire Loyalist army, including the despised Patrick Ferguson. The Patriot losses were small; 28 were killed and 65 wounded. The Loyalist losses were 150 killed, 150 wounded and some 800 captured.

Included among the Patriots killed was Major William Chronicle, but his "South Fork Boys" from present-day Gaston County were victorious.

With the Patriot victory at Kings Mountain, Cornwallis's left flank was destroyed and the British found it harder to muster Loyalists. After subsequent battles at Cowpens and Guilford Courthouse, Cornwallis decided he could not subdue North Carolina. He moved on into Virginia, and in just a little over twelve months after the Battle of Kings Mountain, Cornwallis surrendered to General George Washington and his Continental army on October 19, 1781, at Yorktown, Virginia.

Today the trail that the Overmountain Men traveled is designated a National Historic Trail called the Overmountain Victory Trail and is part of the National Park Service.

The Formation of Gaston County

The early North Carolina counties had no specific western boundaries. New Hanover, established in 1729, included the entire wilderness to the west until Bladen, organized in 1734, fell heir to the western part. Four counties were formed from Bladen in 1748. One was Anson, which embraced all the territory from where Lumberton now stands to the Mississippi River.

In 1762, Mecklenburg was created out of the southern part of Anson. On April 10, 1769, a bill was passed in the North Carolina House of Commons to the effect that all of Mecklenburg County west of the Catawba River would constitute a new county called Tryon. Tryon County was named for Governor William Tryon, who had been appointed governor of the province of North Carolina by the king of England. Before the present boundary line was drawn between North and South Carolina in 1772, the first Tryon County courthouse actually was in York County, South Carolina. After 1772, it was located in present-day Gaston County.

Sometime before the Revolutionary War, Governor Tryon, representing the English Crown, became very unpopular, and a movement was made to do away with the name Tryon County. This occurred in April 1779 when the eastern portion of Tryon County became Lincoln County. By 1840 there was considerable talk of dividing the county.

In 1846 Gaston County was formed from Lincoln County, and got its name from Judge William Joseph Gaston (1778–1844), North Carolina Supreme Court justice and a native of New Bern. Gaston County is bounded on the north by Lincoln County, on the east by the Catawba River, which separates it from Mecklenburg County, on the south by the South Carolina state line and on the west by Cleveland County. Legislation creating the new county required the construction of a courthouse, jail and stocks at the county seat of Dallas.[38] Following the formation and organization of Gaston County, Jesse Holland, who married Martha J. Hanks, the niece of Nancy Hanks, generously donated fifty acres of land

Gaston County was named for William Gaston, a North Carolina Supreme Court judge, who also served in the state House and state Senate. He wrote the state song, "The Old North State." *Courtesy North Carolina State Archives.*

to the county. Of this land, the Dallas courthouse square was set aside and the remainder was sold for building lots. The proceeds for the sale of the lots furnished funds to build the courthouse and jail.

The citizens of Dallas and the new county had no way of knowing that the county seat and the boundary lines for Gaston County would have a way of changing.

Before April of 1915 part of the city of Kings Mountain was in Cleveland County and part in Gaston County. The part in Gaston County was known as East Kings Mountain. According to Gaston County historian Robert Ragan, in a November 12, 2000 article in the *Gastonia Gazette*, a surprise vote by the North Carolina General Assembly in April of 1915 changed the boundary line and put all of the city of Kings Mountain in Cleveland County instead of in Gaston County as some wanted. Gaston County filed a lawsuit insisting that the 1915 vote had been improperly bought with money and whiskey. When another surprise vote was taken, Kings Mountain remained in Cleveland County.

This Greek revival structure in Dallas served as the Gaston County Courthouse from 1848 until 1911, when the county seat was moved to Gastonia. It marks the center of the Dallas Historic District. *Photo by Rita Wehunt-Black.*

This imposing structure was built in 1847 as Gaston County's first jail. The sheriff's family lived on the first floor and prisoners were kept on the second floor. *Photo by Rita Wehunt-Black.*

The following is part of an article about the suit brought against Cleveland County that was printed in the December 23, 1916 issue of the *Gastonia Gazette*:

> *The first real action in the suit Gaston County is bringing against Cleveland County, charging that corruption was practiced in the 1915 county boundary line election, was taken Tuesday afternoon when a bill of complaint was filed, summons issued and the papers forwarded to the sheriff of Cleveland County for service.*
>
> *Attorney N. Fred McMillan, a former citizen of Kings Mountain but now a member of the Gastonia bar, who took an active part in securing the evidence which will more than likely prove damaging to Cleveland County's interests when the case is called in Superior Court, is being severely maligned by a number of citizens of Cleveland County because of his activity in connection with the suit. Mr. McMillan stated to a* Gazette *representative Wednesday that he had been informed by reliable parties that his life had recently been threatened. He stated, however, that he was not worrying over the matter since he had carried on his investigations in a perfectly legitimate way.*

CHAPTER 4

Iron Furnaces and Gold
in Gaston County

The mining of tin, iron and gold was an important part of Gaston County's early history. Iron mining and smelting was prevalent in Gaston County long before towns came into existence.

King George II of England granted a four-hundred-acre tract of land to James Ormand Sr. (1669–1766) in the year 1754 in Old Tryon County, North Carolina. The land was located on Long Creek, adjoining a tract of land on which John Sloan would later build a furnace. The furnace was built around the time of the Revolutionary War and was called Sloan's Furnace.

Sloan's Furnace, two and a half miles west of Bessemer City near a settlement called Vantine on Long Creek, began operating around 1780.[39] Benjamin Ormand bought the furnace in 1827 and the family operated it as the Ormand Furnace. The furnace had to be located on a creek in order to obtain power to operate the triphammer, which was used to beat the ore and improve its texture. The furnace was located only a few hundred yards to the west of the Old Ormand Iron Mining Company. John J. Ormand, who lived in Bessemer City in 1976, was quoted in a 1976 newspaper article as saying,

I have seen quite a few cannon balls about two and a half inches in diameter and a lot of parts of balls as if they failed to fill the moulds full and these pieces could not be used. These half pieces were used for door stops when I was a boy, but they have all been lost or carried away for curios.

Furnaces from that time period made pots, skillets, pans, dog irons, ovens, fire backs and other items needed in the home and on the farm. It is said that cannonballs were made and carried to the Battle of Kings Mountain, but no cannons were used in the battle; the Overmountain Men were moving with such haste that they could not be burdened with any heavy artillery.[40] A few cannonballs of a larger and heavier weight have been found on the battlefield, but they are accounted for by the fact that on October 7, 1880, the War Department sent several units that actually fired for the centennial celebration at Kings

The headstone for Benjamin Ormand Jr. (1791–1853), located in Long Creek Presbyterian Church Cemetery. *Photo by Rita Wehunt-Black.*

Mountain Battlefield. A pen and ink sketch in *Harper's Illustrated Weekly* depicted cannons being fired on that occasion.[41]

A fine school, Buffalo Academy, was founded in the early 1800s near the old Sloan Furnace. An advertisement of 1827 described it as "situated in a healthy place, about 17 miles southwest of Lincolnton, in a respectable and plentiful neighborhood where boarding can be had on ready terms." Patrick J. Sparrow, who had served as a Presbyterian minister at Lincolnton, was principal at Buffalo Academy.[42]

Old-timers recalled, while reminiscing about their youths, visiting the old furnace that they called the Long Creek Furnace in the early twentieth century. They recalled that a man named Dixon was once the overseer at the furnace. They remembered an Englishman named Mr. Hammerskole and a man named Packenstracker working there. A favorite swimming hole was near a waterfall on Long Creek near the furnace.[43] The furnace was abandoned around 1874.

An incident, printed in 1877 by Dr. Cyrus Lee Hunter in *Sketches of Western North Carolina*, relates to the advance of the British army during the Revolution.[44] As Tarleton's cavalry passed through that part of Lincoln County (now Gaston County) they rode up to the home of Benjamin Ormand, on the headwaters of Long Creek, and tied a horse, which had been stolen, to a small oak tree. When Tarleton's cavalry were ready to leave, they took cooking utensils from the kitchen, bedding, blankets and the baby blanket from James Ormand's cradle to use as a saddle blanket. They also took the large Ormand Family Bible (printed in Scotland) to use as a saddle.

The Bible, considerably injured and smeared with blood from the horse's back, was found some time later near Beattie's Ford, on the Catawba River, in the line of the British march, and was returned to the Ormand Family. Alice Webber Cronin, a descendant of Benjamin Ormand stated in 1982 that the Bible was found at Crowders Creek, not the Catawba River.[45]

Ben R. Ormand Jr. writes in his book *Ormand History and Descendants of James Ormand, Sr. 1669–1766* that for many years there was a United States Post Office located near the old furnace called Old Furnace Post Office. The post office was closed shortly after 1902.[46]

The 110th Ormand Family Reunion was held on July 28, 2007, at the Old Furnace Picnic Grounds on Long Creek Road near Bessemer City. The reunion has been held since 1897 at the historic old iron furnace, which is considered to be the oldest stack of its kind in America. The furnace has been designated as a historic property by the Gaston County Historical Commission and Board of Commissioners, and the family has applied to the National Register of Historic Places.

An early iron-smelting furnace was also located in the High Shoals area. John Fulenwider, a Revolutionary War patriot, was the founder of the High Shoals Ironworks around 1795. Iron ore was discovered in the county and a legislative act in 1788 encouraged the building of ironworks in the county. Peter and Abram Forney erected a forge at Big Ore Banks (Irontown Township, Lincoln County), and became pioneers of large-scale iron manufacturing in the state. The iron manufacturing families of the Forneys, Grahams and Brevards were all related through marriage and controlled the industry. John Fulenwider married into this family, and he may have been the most successful of all.

In the late 1790s Fulenwider established the highly successful High Shoals Ironworks where the South Fork River provided the power for a bellows and triphammer to work the ore. He was one of the first producers of pig iron by the charcoal process and of all manufacturers in the county John Fulenwider was the most prosperous and active. During the War of 1812 he contracted with the United States government to make cannonballs.[47]

At the time of his death in 1826, Fulenwider owned some twenty thousand acres of land and a number of slaves. Jacob, the youngest of John's four sons, assumed control of the works after his father's death and increased its output. The High Shoals Ironworks prospered and Jacob Fulenwider added six miles of wooden tracks for the mule-drawn carts that carried the ore from the mines to the foundry.[48]

The Civil War in the 1860s disrupted production, and competition with the other furnaces in the area along with refined steel products marked the end of the iron-producing era in Gaston County.[49]

With the end of iron production as the major industry in Gaston County, other industries took over, especially cotton mills.[50] By 1846, three major cotton mills were operating in Gaston County: the Woodlawn Mill, built by the Lineberger Family; the Stowe Factory, built by the Stowe Family; and the Mountain Island Mill, founded by John R. Tate.[51]

Dave Baity, in his beautiful book *Tracks in Time: A History of the City of Kings Mountain, 1874–2005*, states that at Kings Mountain, by 1840, Ben Briggs had more than eleven thousand acres of land and was engaged in mining the iron ore he had discovered on it.[52] The timber on his land provided wood for the charcoal he used to fire the iron smelter he operated near Pisgah ARP Church at the foot of Crowders Mountain. The iron ore was in a section extending eastward from Kings Mountain toward Crowders Mountain in Gaston County.[53] His iron smelter was at the foot of Crowders Mountain. At one time, Briggs ran a saloon and commissary for the benefit of his employees. It was located in Kings Mountain on the Old Post Road that ran from Lincoln County to Charleston, South Carolina, and at that time it was part of Gaston County. One morning, Mr. Briggs's wife Catherine found a nugget at the bottom of her water bucket at a spring and, when tested, it was found to be a fine grade of gold ore.[54]

Briggs mined his Kings Mountain gold mine for a while, but finding himself unable to handle the costs, he sold his claim to others. After the Civil War, Briggs did not return to North Carolina.[55] The mine changed ownership many times, and at one time a large boardinghouse for miners and their families was built. According to historian Robert Ragan, Briggs's Kings Mountain gold mine attracted miners from England, Germany, Austria, Poland and Italy, and investors from Northern states.

The Lure of Gold in Gaston County

Throughout history the object of man's desire has been gold, and in North Carolina it was no different. Johanne Riedt (Reed) was an illegal immigrant from Germany, a German Hessian soldier who deserted from the British army in Savannah and made his way to the backwoods of Mecklenburg County, North Carolina, where he married Sarah Kiser. He worked on her father's farm.[56] In 1799, in what is today Cabarrus County, their son, twelve-year-old Conrad Reed, found a seventeen-pound shiny yellow rock in Little Meadow Creek while fishing on a Sunday morning. This find would start the nation's first gold rush. The Reed property would become the Reed Gold Mine, which is today the Reed Gold Mine Historic Site.[57] North Carolina was the only gold-producing state in the nation from 1803 until 1828, and it continued to be a leading producer of gold until 1848 when the precious metal was discovered in California.[58] In 1838 the federal government built a branch mint in Charlotte, North Carolina, that coined gold from 1838 until 1861.[59]

Gold has been an important part of Gaston County's history. According to the *Soil Survey of Gaston County* (1989), gold was mined at more than twenty sites in Gaston County along what is known as the Kings Mountain Belt.[60] The Kings Mountain Belt is a narrow, northeast-trending belt of metamorphic rocks that extends for about thirty-five miles. Two types of gold deposits were mined in the western Piedmont, but the hard-rock or lode (veins or mineralized zones) deposits were more prevalent than surface-placer (stream sediment or residual) deposits.[61]

Around 1828, Dr. Elisha Mitchell, North Carolina University's noted geologist and professor of science (for whom Mount Mitchell is named), visited Gaston County to examine gold- and lime-ore deposits and other mineral formations. He wrote in his journal about his adventures and his visit to Kings Creek. He also wrote about meeting William Joseph Wilson and his wife, both of Crowders Creek, when they hosted him in their home.[62] William Joseph Wilson's two-story Flemish-bond brick house, built in 1824, is still standing.[63] Mitchell was also hosted by Fulenwider.[64]

Oliver Mine, believed to be one of the oldest gold mines in Gaston County, is located twelve miles from Charlotte on the west side of the Catawba River. It is thought that this mine was worked prior to the Revolutionary War.

The most important mine in Gaston County was the Kings Mountain Mine (sometimes referred to as the Catawba Mine), in southwestern Gaston County, approximately three miles southeast of the town of Kings Mountain. It was discovered around 1834 and is said to have been worked for forty years. Others say it was worked from 1820 until 1895. The gold was originally discovered in a branch and then the vein was found. Other mines in the Kings Mountain area of Gaston County were the Gap Mine and the Patterson Mine.

The Crowders Mountain (or Caledonia) Mine is located four miles to the east of the Kings Mountain Mine.[65] Work was started here after 1865 and included two shafts.

The Long Creek mine, located eight miles northwest of Gastonia and six miles northwest of Dallas, had three veins: the Asbury, the Dixon and McCarter Hill.

The Duffie Mine is sixteen miles southwest of Charlotte on the Old Tuchaseegee Road. This gold mine had a small trace of silver.

Other gold mines were the Reese, Clemmer, McClurd, Oliver and Robinson Mines in the northeast part of the county. In the southeast part of Gaston County were the Lineberger Mine near Cramerton, the Wright Mine on Catawba Creek and the Eddleman and Dameron Mines.

Originally known as Brevard Station, the town of Stanley was also known for gold. In 1854 its name was changed to Stanley for gold prospector Colonel Stanley and the nearby creek where he found small amounts of gold.

The Carter Hill Gold Mine near Pasour's Mountain was said to have been profitable because of the excellent condition of the gold.

Some insight into gold mining in the early 1900s in Gaston County can be gained from the newspaper article printed in the *Cherryville Eagle* on November 15, 1917, concerning the sale of the Long Creek Gold Mine:

Long Creek Gold Mine Sold to Mr. D.E. Rhyne for $35,000 Cash

Some weeks ago it was announced in this paper that Mr. John J. George had sent a telegram in Richmond and reached home before the telegram. It was not known at the time what business he had in Richmond that necessitated such speed. It has since leaked out that other parties were interested in the purchase of the Long Creek Gold Mine property, and that Mr.

George, at the request of Mr. Rhyne, closed the deal, and authorized the draft on Mr. Rhyne for $35,000 cash.

This is one the largest real estate deals put through in this county for some time, and Mr. Rhyne becomes the owner of a very valuable tract of land. The property consists of 600 acres fine timberland. With the land, go all the mining interests, buildings, machinery, and concentrates. It is understood that Mr. Rhyne intends to develop this magnificent property and that mining operations will soon begin.

Years ago this property was successfully mined, and the other settlers tell wonderful stories about great quantities of gold that have been taken from this property, and that mining operations will soon begin.

Mr. Rhyne is one of the wealthiest and best businessmen in this section of the state, and he is abundantly able to develop this property and test out its value; and we are glad that he has become the purchaser of it.

It is understood that he is going to cut and saw much of this valuable timber at once; and it is hinted around here that he has become interested in another modern cotton mill erected here in town or very near town.

Just what interest Mr. George may have in the mine, if any, is not known but we learn that he is going to be associated with Mr. Rhyne in the development of this gold mine property, which he almost sold about a year ago for $100,000. This is the price that we hear the parties have placed on the purchase. Mr. George says he shipped ore from the mine that averaged $27 per ton, and he is much pleased at the purchase.

Saint Joseph's Catholic Church and the Irish Gold Miners

Saint Joseph's Catholic Church located on North Carolina Highway 273 was built by Irish immigrants who came to Gaston County in search of gold. They had heard of the discovery of gold on the nearby banks of the Catawba River and came to Gaston County to work in the gold mines. The government closed the mines in 1832, and some of the Irish immigrants stayed in the area. They wanted a Catholic Church to serve their religious needs. According to Clip Johnson, Reverend J.J. O'Connell, a circuit priest who traveled by horseback throughout the Carolinas and parts of Georgia, held infrequent Masses for the tiny congregation until Bishop John England of Charleston assigned Reverend T.J. Cronin to serve the Catholics in the area.[66]

Carl Heil, historian and caretaker for the church, states that when O'Connell retired and the church closed, he bought land six miles to the south in Belmont on which he built a home and farm. The Benedictine Monks, named for Saint Benedict who lived fifteen hundred years ago, asked O'Connell to sell the land to them for a college and monastery. He agreed, on the condition that he could continue to live there and be buried there on holy ground at his death. Belmont Abbey College opened in 1876.[67]

The church at Belmont Abbey was completed in 1893, and was once the only abbey cathedral in the nation. In 1998 it was named a minor basilica by Rome, a rare papal honor. It is located on the 650-acre campus of Belmont Abbey College. Its beautiful stained-glass windows won a gold prize at the Colombian Exposition in 1893. The

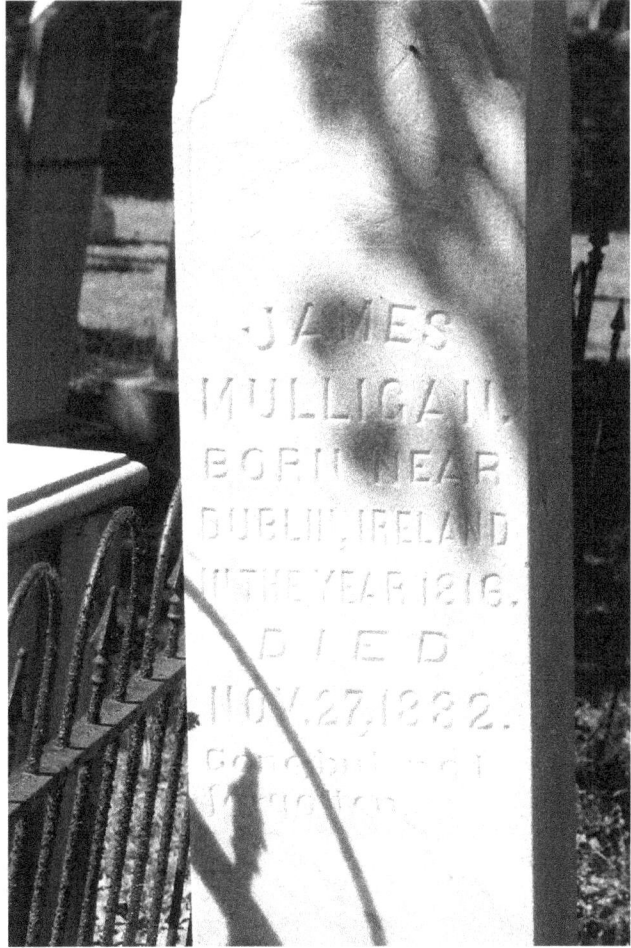

Built in 1843 for Irish immigrant gold miners, Saint Joseph's Catholic Church was dedicated by Bishop I.A. Reynolds, doctor of divinity of the diocese of Charleston, South Carolina. It is the oldest standing Catholic church in the state. *Photo by Rita Wehunt-Black.*

central campus has been designated a historic district on the National Register of Historic Places.

The church contains a stone baptismal font, which legend says was first used by Native Americans in the Belmont area and later served as a slave block where slaves were sold. When the monks arrived in 1876, they named the monastery "Mariastein" (Mary Stone) in recognition of the stone's prominence. On the stone is a plaque that reads, "Upon this rock men once were sold into slavery. Now upon this rock, through the waters of Baptism, men become free children of God."

Belmont Abbey Cathedral was once the only abbey cathedral in the nation. It was completed in 1893, and was named a minor basilica by Rome. *Photo by Rita Wehunt-Black.*

CHAPTER 5

Taking the Waters

Native Americans were probably the first humans to see Crowders Mountain and the mineral springs located there. The Crowders Mountain area was once within the borders of the Catawba Indian Nation. Although Native American artifacts have been found near the springs, we don't know the role the springs played in the Catawba Indians' lives.[68] However, what we do know about the mineral springs is a fascinating story.

During the late 1800s, Dr. Francis M. Garrett of eastern North Carolina built and managed a private health resort at All Healing Springs, which is located northeast of Crowders Mountain. Like many physicians of his day, Dr. Garrett believed that drinking and bathing in mineral waters could help disease.[69]

An archaeological survey and testing program was started in 1995 to clear the area around the springs, recover artifacts and information about the resort and school and map the area. A report entitled *Taking the Waters: All Healing Springs Spa and Nineteenth-Century Homeopathy* written by Dr. J. Alan May describes the results of the survey, along with a historical overview, and was published in 2002 in *North Carolina Archaeology*.[70] Dr. May's complete report is a "must-read" for anyone interested in the history of Crowders Mountain, All Healing Springs and Linwood College. Dr. May opens his report with this abstract:

Within the southern Piedmont of North Carolina are a number of streams and springs as well as a temperate climate. During the latter half of the nineteenth century there arose an interest in homeopathic medicine and related cures. Principal among these were healing springs and water treatments. Local entrepreneurs built a hotel/resort in western Gaston County, North Carolina near Crowders Mountain to cater to an increasingly affluent local populace. An archaeological survey and testing program was undertaken to recover artifacts and information about the resort. Several foundations associated with the spa-hotel, dormitory, and residence were identified and collected. Much of the area has returned to secondary growth forest and identifying spring and building sites described in the literature was difficult. Two cisterns along with the principal springs were relocated, cleared of debris, and mapped.

Born in Connecticut, Emily
Catherine Prudden (1832–1917)
died in Hickory, North Carolina,
after devoting her entire life
to others. *Courtesy G.A. Pfeiffer
Library, Pfeiffer University.*

According to Mike Peters and Dr. May's extensive deed research, Benjamin Briggs of South Carolina, beginning in August 1852, began purchasing large tracts of land including Crowders Mountain and All Healing Springs from the original land grant owners for the timber and iron ore he thought underlay much of this area of Gaston County. Dr. Garrett was one of five brothers who, in 1863, purchased 9,526 acres from Samuel Oakes, Peter Baxter and A.R. Homesley for $6,500. The Garrett brothers held the property, which included All Healing Springs, until around 1880 when they built the All Healing Springs Health and Pleasure Resort. They were joined in this venture by R.Y. McAden, a textile mill owner, who would later develop the mill town of McAdenville on the South Fork River. Promotional brochures marketed All Healing Springs Health and Pleasure Resort as having been "proved by trial to exercise a curative influence on almost all diseases of the human system," including throat diseases, bleeding piles, skin diseases, dyspepsia, general debility, constipation, rheumatism, gout and uterine diseases.[71]

When opened on June 1, 1881, the resort consisted of the Mountain View Hotel and twelve mineral spring bathing and drinking areas. This resort quickly grew, and by 1884 the resort had its own post office, nearby merchants, private residences and farms. Dr. Garrett sold small plots adjacent to his resort where the owners built small cottages. The cottage owners had to sign a deed stating that all meals would be taken at the Mountain View Hotel.[72]

On July 25, 1884, the Mountain View Hotel was severely damaged in a fire that originated in the kitchen. The hotel reopened in May 1885, and by 1888 the resort had not only been completely rebuilt, but also had been expanded. In addition to a new hotel and cottages, the resort now included a large amusement pavilion with billiards, a tenpin alley and a gymnasium with space for rollerskating and bicycle riding. Adjoining the gym was a ballroom with twenty-four hundred feet of floor space for dancing. Walking trails to the summit of Crowders Mountain and outdoor sports facilities were also added.[73]

From an educational standpoint, Dr. Garrett's most significant contribution to the region was providing the land for a school for young ladies that would become Linwood College. The school was the idea of Miss Emily C. Prudden of Orange, Connecticut. She was fifty-two years old, profoundly deaf and suffered from severe arthritis when she arrived in Gaston County. This marked the start of her thirty-year pilgrimage of establishing fifteen schools for poor children across western North and South Carolina. One of the schools that Miss Prudden started would become Pfeiffer College in Misenheimer, North Carolina.

On October 18, 1884, Garrett sold Miss Prudden fifty acres adjacent to All Healing Springs for just one dollar in order that she might build a school for poor young women and train them to be local schoolteachers. In 1884, Prudden Hall, the first building built at the school, was opened under Miss Prudden's direction. After receiving financial backing from Judge Edwin S. Jones, more new buildings were constructed at the school. In 1886, two years after she started the school in Gaston County, Miss Prudden opened another school in Blowing Rock, North Carolina, known as Skyland Institute. In 1888, she transferred the land deed to Judge Jones and the school became Jones Seminary and later Jones Seminary and Institute.[74]

In 1888, she opened Lincoln Academy at All Healing Springs as a boarding school for black children in Gaston County. This was one of seven schools that she would open to educate black students. Many graduates of Lincoln Academy went on to become doctors, lawyers and other professionals. John Biggers, an internationally known artist, graduated from Lincoln Academy. In 1955, Lincoln Academy became part of the Gaston County School System and was moved to Bessemer City where it became Lincoln High School.[75]

In 1904, Archie Thomas Lindsay, a local Presbyterian minister, purchased the All Healing Springs Health and Pleasure Resort and Jones Seminary. He combined these facilities to create an expanded coeducational college of which he served as president. At the suggestion of his students, Lindsay renamed the school Linwood College; "Lin" from Lindsay and "wood" from the wooded mountain slopes surrounding the college.

In 1914 Linwood College became a four-year, degreed, coeducational institution with continued provision for Bible study, and the campus included 138 acres of land. Linwood College remained open until 1921. The Greek Orthodox Church took ownership in 1926

Mr. and Mrs. P.L. Lacour, Mrs. A.L. Mauney and Miss S.A. Sadguiar taught in area Rosenwald Schools for African Americans around 1910. They were started by Sears & Roebuck executive Julius Rosenwald. Rosenwald Teacherage was in Belmont. *Courtesy Cherryville Museum.*

and began operating it as a monastery, primary school and orphanage. The facility was finally abandoned in 1930.

All that was not carried away through the years from the All Healing Springs and Linwood College site is documented in the lengthy archaeological survey written by Dr. J. Alan May. Besides the two rock cisterns, the following is only a small portion of what was gleaned from the site during the archaeological survey: one auto battery cell cap; two black ceramic doorknob fragments; two red phonograph record fragments; one metal roof tab disk; one clockwork (incomplete); one large metal tack; one fragment wire; nine metal hangers; one metal door hinge; seven auto battery (Ford) fragments; and one broken "shot" glass. Several fragments of white graniteware (chamber pot remains) were recovered from the dump, Hotel/Jones Hall and Prudden Hall.[76]

Bessemer City and Mysterious Whetstone Mountain

A Lilac bush and an Apple tree
Were standing in the woods
Out on the hill above the town,
Where once a farmhouse stood.
In the winter the leaves are bare
And no one sees the signs
Of a house that stood and a garden that grew
And life in another time.

One Spring when the buds came bursting forth
And grass grew on the land,
The Lilac spoke to the Apple tree
As only an old friend can.
Do you think, said the Lilac, this might be the year
When someone will build here once more?
Here by the cellar, still open and deep,
There's room for new walls and a floor.

Oh no, said the Apple, there are so few
Who come here on the mountain this way
And when they do, they don't often see
Why we're growing here, so far away.
A long time ago we were planted by hands
That worked in the mines and the mills
When the country was young and the people
who came
Built their homes in the hills.

But now there are cities, the roads have come
And no one lives here today
And the only signs of the farms in the hills
Are the things not carried away.
Broken dishes, piles of boards,
A tin plate, an old leather shoe.
And an Apple tree still bending down
And a Lilac where a garden once grew.[77]

Long before Bessemer City was chartered on March 6, 1893, iron ore had been mined there for decades and several iron furnaces operated in the area. These supplied the ore for the Fulenwider Ironworks at High Shoals, which could be reached by a horse-powered tramway.[78] The railroad stop was called Wooten Station. A second stop, west of Whetstone Mountain, was called Vantine. Located nearby were Wooten's General Store and the area that would later be named Whetstone Mountain. Wooten Station was the stop where many guests would disembark and take a buggy to All Healing Springs Hotel at Crowders Mountain. In fact, the first post office to serve the Bessemer City area was called Crowders Mountain Post Office. Some wanted to call the little settlement Piney Top, because of the abundance of pine trees in the area, but when all the trees were cut by loggers, a few called it Stump Town.

The Richmond and Danville Railroad Company had built a rail line through the area, and in 1871 the Atlanta and Charlotte Division of the company extended the tracks from the Gastonia Station to Wooten Station before heading toward Cleveland and on down through South Carolina. As the tracks curved northward, the builders had to slice through a rock-studded elevation rich in whetstone. It took a year to dig through the mountain using picks, shovels and mules, and laying the rails through Whetstone Mountain was considered an engineering feat at the time. One digger remarked that there were enough whetstones "to sharpen a scythe for every man on the face of the earth!"[79] Thus, Whetstone Mountain got its name.

In the early pioneer days of the area that today surrounds Bessemer City, early settlers heard wolves and wildcats howl at night on Whetstone Mountain and saw foxfire glow in the lowlands, giving rise to speculation about ghosts, fireballs and other mysterious goings-on. One story by the late Mr. Fred Arrowood recalled that when Jim Edwards worked on the railroad there, he had knocked on the Arrowood's door one evening and asked to spend the night. Edwards explained that, as he was riding in the dark along Whetstone Mountain, a catamount or mountain lion had started stalking him and his horse, crying like a woman and making his horse skittish and Jim nervous, so he had decided to take refuge.[80] Another story tells of a haunted well at the Old Clemmer Place, later bought by the Moss family.[81]

The town of Bessemer City got its start when Reidsville tobacco manufacturer John A. Smith had surveyor W.R. Richardson lay out the town with streets, avenues and three public parks. Most agree that John A. Smith named the town, choosing Bessemer City because, when he had first arrived, the ore being mined was known as Bessemer iron. The "Bessemer Process" for mass-producing steel from iron ore was named for the Englishman, Sir Henry Bessemer (1813–1898), who invented this process. He was knighted in 1879 for his contributions to science. Mr. Smith was known to have a large ego, and people could not believe that he did not name the town Smithville or Smithtown after himself. Later, some new parents would choose the name Bessemer for their infant girls.

In 1891, John A. Smith sent out a "Prospectus of the Bessemer City Mining and Manufacturing Company, Bessemer City, N.C." to prospective investors. It pictured Bessemer as a paradise on Earth, situated in the great mineral belt, and stated:

> *The company proposes to develop its vast and numerous deposits of fine Bessemer iron ore. Owing to the fact that our ores are of a high Bessemer Grade, and average over 60 percent metallic iron, we can ship them at a handsome profit. This coupled with our lime quarries, granite quarries, and sale of town lots, will make the stock of the Bessemer City Mining and Manufacturing Company one of the safest and best dividend-paying stocks in the south.*

> *The town-lot property comprises 1,778 acres and the large and handsome two-hundred room hotel, to cost fifty to $100,000, is now being erected, and will be opened for guests on December 1, 1891. It is situated on top of Whetstone Mountain, 125 feet above the railroad track; but is gradual that a horse carrying two people in a buggy can trot comfortably to horse and occupants from the depot to the hotel door. A prominent hotelist says our new hotel can be filled to overflowing (even with 500 rooms) by northern visitors in winter and southern visitors in summer.*

Smith had an ingenious arrangement of buckets, wires and windlasses to take water from the cool spring below up the mountain to the hotel.[82]

> *Mr. W.R. Richardson, the civil engineer who surveyed Bessemer City, says there is no view near Asheville that will compare with the view at Bessemer City. The intention of the Company now is to have its first lot sale the last of October or first of November, 1891. Two saw and planning mills, sash, door, and blind factories, plus a shoe factory have already been guaranteed.[83]*

Smith continues with a geographical and historical overview of the area:

> *The property is situated in Gaston County, N.C., six miles north-west of Kings Mountain, N.C., and twenty-eight miles south-west of Charlotte, N.C. This is one of the finest farming counties in North Carolina. Here cotton grows to perfection. Gaston County has three railroads, several large colleges for both male and females, and already 14 or 15 cotton factories in operation. So it will be seen at a glance that you are not going to a wild and poverty-stricken county to invest your money. Bessemer City, it must be remembered, is one of the healthiest and most picturesque places in Western North Carolina. In short it is the garden spot of Western North Carolina. Bessemer is situated on a high plateau 1,250 feet above the level of the sea, overlooking a space of country as far as the eye will reach, embracing all or a part of ten counties. No Malaria or mosquitoes ever known here on the south side of the Blue Ridge. No piercing fogs and there is coming a sanitarium for consumptives and all weak lunged people and asthmatic sufferers. Overlooking the battle-ground where the celebrated battle of King's Mountain was fought in the Revolutionary War where the hardy militia of the mountains literally massacred the British General Ferguson and his army.*

The prospectus continues, detailing the battle for several glowing paragraphs, and includes that

> *within one mile, and in sight of the new hotel, stands the old [Ormand] blast furnace used for making cannon balls during the Revolutionary War, many of which are found here now. The ores used in this furnace were the finest in the world and the same mines which have lain idle since 1792 are now owned by the Bessemer City Company.[84]*

In 1894 a typhoid fever epidemic swept through Gaston County. Coincidentally, a new coffin company had just opened in the town of Gastonia, which gave work to a crew of unemployed carpenters and joiners.[85] In spite of the epidemic, All Healing Springs Resort continued to operate.[86]

John Smith's plan for a resort town was unsuccessful and his hotel, much smaller than anticipated, was gone by 1912. Not to be defeated, Smith built the town's first cotton mill in 1895, called the Southern Cotton Mills. Bessemer City was unusual in that the mill village system was not as strong as in the rest of the county, probably due to the presence of working-class homes prior to the establishment of the mills.[87]

Mining returned to the Bessemer City area in 1954 when some rich veins of lithium were discovered near Bessemer City and the Lithium Corporation of America built a plant there.

Simon Hager (1763–1835)

Simon Hager was born at Hager's Ferry in Tryon County, North Carolina, on the east side of Killian's Creek, in 1763. He was the son of Johann George Hager (an immigrant from Germany) and wife Crate Killian. At the age of seventeen, he enlisted in Captain William Hutchinson's company of Colonel Polk's regiment and served ten months as a Patriot in the Revolutionary War, after which he was pensioned. He served mainly in South Carolina and was engaged in the Battle of Moncks Corner and Eutaw Springs. Simon Hager's land was in the Long Creek section of Gaston County, near present-day Bessemer City. Simon married Elizabeth Lawing some time after 1785 and they had seven known children. These seven named in his will are Frederick Hager, John Hager, Jackson Hager, Katherine Hager, William Hager (who inherited his land), Barbara Hager and Mary Hager.

One Hager-published genealogy says that Simon Hager is buried in a Presbyterian church cemetery, but descendants of Simon who still live on the old Hager property near Bessemer City say he is buried in the Hager family cemetery on the Hager property. Janet Neal Brown, librarian at Bessemer City Library, and great-great-great-granddaughter of Simon Hager, states that her father Clyde Neal, who farmed the property, said that Simon Hager was buried in the Hager family cemetery near the old homesite and spring. There was also a slave cemetery next to the Hager cemetery. A thimble and bits of pottery found at the site were once in Clyde Neal's possession.

"The Other Simon Hager"

Occasionally, Simon Hager of Long Creek is confused with another Simon Hager (1755–1843), who was known as "Big" Simon Hager to distinguish him from the Long Creek Simon Hager. "Big" Simon Hager also fought in the Revolutionary War and marched with his Whig neighbors. He first enlisted in Captain Peter Sides's company and served four months. He later enlisted in Captain John Baker's company and served three months, after which he served in Salisbury and then in South Carolina. When the cause of liberty seemed hopeless, "Big" Simon Hager was persuaded by some of his Tory acquaintances to join Colonel Ferguson at Kings Mountain. At the end of the Battle of Kings Mountain, Hager was taken prisoner. He was recognized by Abram Forney, his neighbor and a member of the Lincoln County troops. Forney exclaimed: "Is that you, Simon?"

"Yes," Hager replied quickly, "it is, Abram, and I beg you to get me out of this bullpen; if you do, I will promise never to be caught in such a scrape again."

At "Big" Simon Hager's trial, he was set free and, true to his word, soon afterwards he joined his former Whig comrades and marched to the Battle of Guilford Courthouse. He was a good soldier to the end of the war. He was even pensioned, and he died on December 27, 1843, at the age of ninety. He is buried at Henkle's (Old White Haven) Church.[88]

William J. Hager (born in 1802) was the son of Simon Hager, the Revolutionary War Patriot who lived near Long Creek. They are both buried in the Old Hager Cemetery near Bessemer City. *Courtesy Janet Neal Brown.*

CHAPTER 6

The German Migration

Beyond the Blue Mountains

German immigrants of the 1700s came from the war-ravaged areas along the Rhine River. Mostly they were all lumped together and called "Palatines," because the majority of them really did come from the Palatinate (Pfalz). But they also came from parts of Switzerland, Baden, Wurttemberg, Alsace, the Rhineland, Hessen and Westphalia.[89]

Around 1708, an agent of William Penn visited the Palatine area of Germany along the Rhine River and encouraged these Germans to immigrate to William Penn's colony in the New World. They traveled down the Rhine River and boarded ships at the Port of Rotterdam in Holland. While America was still made up of colonies of Great Britain, all immigrant ships to colonial ports had to be English. In 1709, the first shiploads of German immigrants had reached England. Queen Anne provided food and temporary housing in tents for the homeless Germans and farm implements for when they would eventually leave for the colonies of New York and Pennsylvania. The bulk of Germans came into the port of Philadelphia, although the 1709 group came into the port of New York.

After arriving in Pennsylvania, the Germans soon felt the hostility of the English and Welsh Quakers who had earlier sought religious freedom in Pennsylvania. Secretary James Logan, himself a Scotsman, on March 25, 1727, wrote to William Penn's son in England with another complaint about the Germans:

> *We have many thousands of foreigners, most Palatines so-called, already in ye country, of whom near 1500 came in this last summer; many of them are a surly people, divers papists among them, and ye men generally well arm'd.*

At the same time many Scots-Irish, former Scottish families who had moved from their homeland to establish the linen trade in Ireland, now found themselves unable to cope with English taxes and joined the migration to Pennsylvania. Secretary Logan, who in 1724 had written about the "bold and indigent stranger" from Ireland, wrote again to John Penn in 1724 to complain about the feisty Scots-Irish:

> *Eight or nine ships this last from Newcastle. Both of these sorts* [Germans and Scotsmen] *sit frequently down on any spot of vacant Land they can find, without asking questions; the last Palatines say there will be twice the number next year, and ye Irish say ye same of their people.*

As German and Scots-Irish settlers pressed against the Allegheny Mountains of Central Pennsylvania in need of land, they had two choices. The first was to cross the mountains into western Pennsylvania.[90] The understandable reluctance of the Native Americans to sell their land, and their violent reaction to settlers, made most choose the second option: they would move southward to the Virginia and Carolina backcountry. There would be no boundary disputes there such as the Pennsylvania-Maryland dispute. Many who were involved in the "Digges Choice" dispute in the Conewago settlement, in what is today the southeastern part of Adams County, Pennsylvania, on the Maryland border, migrated to the Piedmont of North Carolina.[91]

Through years of research into German history, I have often wondered why the Scots-Irish and German immigrants seemed to get along so well throughout the settling of America, and intermarry so freely, even though the Lutheran pastors had warned, "It is seldom that German and English blood is happily united in wedlock." The temperaments of these two ethnic groups were so different that sometimes it was heard among the Germans, "Shouldn't have ever gotten mixed up with the Irish!"

James L. Haney Jr., in *Stumbling toward Zion: A Mosteller Chronicle*, tells the consequences of Michael and Anna Maria Mosteller's move from their Germanic-speaking community in Lincoln County to McDowell County, North Carolina, in the 1850s. Michael's daughter, Margaret Rebecca Mosteller, changed her name to "Peggy" and became pregnant.[92] Peggy had been going out with some of the "English" boys. Michael Mosteller refused to let his other two daughters leave the farm, but they outwitted their father. They escaped to go to a wild Election Day celebration where they too became pregnant.[93] Their father declared that he would not allow his daughters to marry these "no good English" boys. He also accused his son of being just like the "English" boys.[94]

It took delving into Scots-Irish history to understand. After reading about the all-too-familiar prejudices aimed at the Scots-Irish (which I knew had also been aimed at the German immigrants) I began to understand. Since linguistic differences stimulated bigotry, there was great pressure in the colonies to speak English. Because of their Scots-Gaelic dialect, the Scots-Irish could be easily identified as linguistically alien.[95]

Germans were not only alienated by language from English-speaking ethnic groups, but some were also separated by dialects from each other. In the Shenandoah Valley the Germans developed a trade jargon called "Valley Dutch" in order to communicate across ethnic boundaries, while at the same time retaining their individual dialects in their homes. Later, Germans would fight on both sides of the Revolutionary War in the Catawba Valley.

One soldier observed in his diary, "Ofttimes one of our German soldiers could be seen leaning on his rifle, listening to the sounds of his mother tongue as they were wafted over from the enemy's camp."

Even the tolerant Benjamin Franklin was disturbed by the newcomers, and he wrote in 1751:

> Why should the Palatine boors be suffered to swarm into our settlements, and by herding together, establish their language and manners, to the exclusion of ours? Why should Pennsylvania, founded by the English, become a colony of aliens, who will shortly be so numerous as to Germanize us, instead of our Anglicifying them, and will never adopt our language or customs any more than they will acquire our complexion?...Ben Franklin, 1751

Franklin later explained rather weakly that by "boor" he meant "farmer."

Settling at first around Philadelphia, the Germans and Scots-Irish slowly spread west and south. First they moved to Lancaster and York Counties in Pennsylvania, and then into Maryland, often acting as a buffer for the English against the Native Americans to the west. The accusation was made and heard often in colonial times that the English, who had settled along the Atlantic coastal plain, wanted Scots-Irish and Germans to stay where they were as buffers against the frontier "Indians." Fear of attack by Native Americans, especially the Iroquois to the north, encouraged many Germans to move south. German settlers in the Colebrook Valley in 1728 petitioned the governor for better protection against the savages.

In Berks County, Pennsylvania, during 1755–57, at the time of the French and Indian War, many of the settlers had good cause to be frightened. The Native Americans had broken the barrier of the Blue Mountains and were raiding almost at will the farms of Allemengel, Berne, Tulpehocken, Bethel and Swatara. In Lancaster, the courthouse bell rang almost constantly throughout the day on October 28, 1755, to call the people together to defend themselves. The Jacob Hochstetler family massacre in Berks County took place in October of 1757, after an evening gathering of young people who were assisting in paring and slicing apples for drying. Other sources give a June 1754 date for a Hostetter family massacre (Bern) in Berks County.[96]

I first read about the Clemmer Massacre around 1980 at the York County Historical Society in York, Pennsylvania. The massacre took place at or near Baker's Ridge in Frederick County, Maryland. The Clemmer (Klemmer) family was on their way back from burying a child when they had two boys abducted—George Valentine ("Felty") and Lawrence. George Valentine "Felty" Clemmer was born in 1747 in York County, Pennsylvania (not in Germany as some sources say). He was born at the Conewago Settlement near Littlestown and was the son of Johann Ludwig Clemmer from Friedelsheim, Germany.[97] Felty was nine years old and his brother was seven when their father was killed and they were captured along with their mother who was later killed. The Native Americans then moved their captives to Wills Mountain near Cumberland, Maryland. The boys were held captive for more than eight years, from August 20, 1756, until November of 1764, and it is believed that they spent the majority of that time in present-day Ohio. At the end of the French and Indian War the boys were returned to the white settlers.

Felty Clemmer married Elizabeth Dottero (Tutherow) in Pennsylvania, and after her death, he married Margaretha Wigand. The Wigand Family had also come from the village of Friedelsheim and the village of Freinsheim in Germany. The Hostetters (Huffstetlers), the Johann Friederich Wigand (Wehunt) family and others were at Christ (German) Reformed Church (present-day Adams County, Pennsylvania, near Littlestown), when Felty had been baptized in 1747 by Reverend Michael Schlatter.

After Valentine "Felty" Clemmer's death in Pennsylvania, Margaretha Wigand Clemmer migrated to Rowan County, North Carolina, with other members of the Clemmer family and the Johann Friederich Wigand family around 1787, and then eventually arrived in the Long Creek area of Lincoln County (present-day Gaston County).

William Penn's son tried hard to stop the migration of the German people, but it was too late; they had already established themselves as part of the fabric of the New World. Once they were out of Pennsylvania, and after finding fertile farmland farther south, the talent of the Germans as farmers became obvious. Daniel Dulany, a prominent Marylander, wrote to Governor Samuel Ogle in 1745:

> *You would be surprised to see how much the country is improved beyond the mountains, especially by the Germans, who are the best people that can be to settle a wilderness; and the fertility of the soil makes them ample amends for their industry.*

Later, Governor Charles Eden sent a report home to England stating that the Germans' extraordinary industry had raised the spirit of emulation among the other inhabitants, and that they were a most useful people who merited the public regard, acknowledged by all who were acquainted with them.

The Germans would later be recognized not only for their skill at farming, but also for their talents as master furniture craftsmen, watchmakers, wagon makers, gunsmiths, shoemakers, cordwainers, blacksmiths, silversmiths, millwrights and carpenters and for the education of their children in the home and later by Lutheran clergy sent from Germany.

Those of us descended from German ancestors, who came into Pennsylvania in the 1700s from the Palatinate, Württemburg and other countries bordering along the Rhine River, are a strange breed. No matter how many generations removed, our ears are greeted pleasantly when we hear the German language spoken here in the U.S. or in Europe. Even if we do not speak fluent German, the familiarities are overwhelming, and in an instant all those generations between us are gone and one has that calm feeling of home and belonging. Growing up in the 1950s and early '60s, German words, such as *receipt* for recipe, *haus* for house and *counterpane* for bedspread were still spoken in some homes in Lincoln, Catawba and Gaston Counties. Some of us were even corrected by well-meaning teachers, who informed us quietly that we were not using the correct words—and so "the King's English" prevailed.

The Pennsylvania-German dialect, known as "Pennsylvanisch-Deutsch," lingered long after the German settlers came to North Carolina. The misnomer that these people were originally from Holland, and thus Dutch, is still alive today. Because the immigrants had to travel up the Rhine River to Rotterdam in Holland before crossing the Atlantic, some said that they had left from Holland, and people thought they were Dutch. When asked by their English-speaking neighbors what kind of people they were, they replied, "Deutcsch" (German), and soon they were referred to as Pennsylvania-Dutch.[98] There was a saying among the early families descended from German ancestors who were called "the Dumb Dutch" by some English at the time: "We are not dumb, and we are not Dutch!"

The Germans had names that were hard to pronounce. Some Germans anglicized them, but usually they were anglicized for them, or just written down the way they sounded by the English officials. Very few Germans owned slaves, but those who did spoke and taught German to their slaves. During the American Revolution, the language barrier probably hindered those of German extraction, but they certainly were not considered as a whole to be Loyalists.[99]

The Peiter Heyl Memorial Monument, erected near Dallas, North Carolina, on August 11, 1938, by the Hoyle family, was moved to Kadesh Church in Cleveland County in 1960. *Photo by Rita Wehunt-Black.*

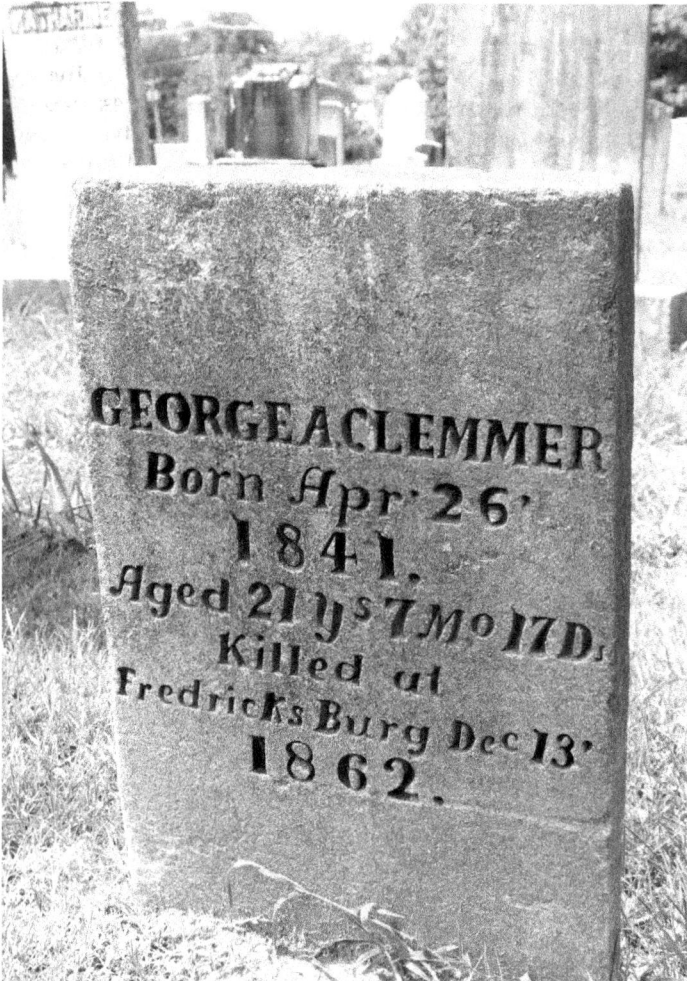

George A. Clemmer, who died during the Civil War, is buried in the Lutheran Chapel Church Cemetery on New Hope Road in Gastonia. *Photo by Rita Wehunt-Black.*

It is said that in the Catawba Valley, in Lincoln and Catawba Counties, German was still spoken in some of the churches up until the 1900s. A traveler in North Carolina in the 1800s might have worshiped on Sundays in churches where the services were still conducted entirely in German, in which both the Lutheran and German reformed had equal rights and privileges, and each denomination worshiped on alternate Sundays. These churches were known as "Union Churches," and the hymn book in use would have been the ever-present *Gemainshaftliches Gesangbuch*, the union hymn book. At one side of the church, there would have stood the high goblet-shaped pulpit, with a sounding board suspended over the head of the officiating minister. A few are still preserved in North Carolina and they are still common today in Germany. Outside the church would have been found fine, well-bred horses and well-made buggies.

Black Powder

We will rise and warm our eyes
And bless our hearts, for the old year's gone
And the New Year's come
And for good luck, we'll fire our guns.
—from Chant of the New Year Shooters

The German settlers of Gaston County clung tenaciously to their language, their Lutheran religion, their German foods and their customs for as long as possible. One of the most interesting cultural carry-overs from Germany that has not died out and has ushered in the New Year for well over two hundred years is the custom of "Shooting in the New Year," as it is called.

In and around the Cherryville area, in northwestern Gaston County, black powder and the roar of muskets, the sound traveling for miles, mark the end of one year and the beginning of another. Starting at midnight on New Year's Eve, these descendants of German and Scots-Irish settlers travel the highways and back roads of Gaston County and some parts of Cleveland and Lincoln Counties calling on families and businesses throughout the night and all through New Year's Day wishing them well and shooting their guns to announce the New Year until sundown. After the "Greeting" or "Chant," each reveler fires a round of his musket to wish luck for the individuals. Even with television crews recording for the next evening's news it is a unique and magical sight. Black powder is poured down the barrel of the old muskets, the ramrod is unscrewed and the powder tapped and then a cap, which makes the spark ignite the powder, is put into place. The musket is then held away from the body by the stock before the trigger is pulled. Afterwards the shooters are invited in for strong coffee, ginger tea, homemade wine, cigars or a complete meal.

One of the most interesting features of the custom is the "Chant" handed down through generations from one "Speech Crier" to the next, usually father to son. The custom is definitely from Germany, but the Cherryville chant sounds to some to be almost out of Old England. In Cherryville, A. Sidney Beam (1872–1960), a descendant of the immigrant John Teeter Beam, gave the chant for over sixty years starting in 1889. He learned the chant one fall from his two brothers, Jacob and Lee Beam, while picking cotton.

The origin of the chant is not known, but Jan Harold Brunvard in *The Study of American Folklore* states,

> *The custom has elements in it of English mummers plays and the custom of belsnickles and shanghais followed in the late nineteenth century in Virginia, and a dim parallel perhaps in the traditional Southern holiday greeting "Christmas Gift!"*

A similar German chant from Lehigh County, Pennsylvania, was translated from its original German in 1972 by Harold Hass before it was lost forever.

The New Year Shooters pose in January of 1913 on the front porch of the Stephen Homesley House. The house is located on South Pink Street in Cherryville. Homesley, a German immigrant, built the house in 1810 near a spring. *Courtesy Cherryville Historical Museum.*

Thundering muskets herald in the New Year during the annual celebration. *Courtesy Cherryville Historical Museum.*

Black powder is used by the New Year Shooters in their muskets, flintlock rifles and breechloaders. *Courtesy Cherryville Historical Museum.*

E.G. Green is delivering the chant for the Cherryville New Year Shooters as they shoot in the New Year in this undated photograph. *Courtesy Cherryville Historical Museum.*

New Year Shooters W. Blaine Beam and Sidney Beam are ready for a radio broadcast at the home of Ruffin White in the 1940s. *Courtesy Cherryville Historical Museum.*

Mummers are simply costumed entertainers welcoming in the New Year. Some of the earliest mummers date back to ancient Egypt. The tradition was also practiced by the Romans in the Roman Festival of Saturnalias where Latin laborers marched in masks throughout the day of satire and gift giving. This included Celtic variations of "trick-or-treat" and Druidic noisemaking to drive away demons for the New Year. The early Swedish mummers appointed a leader, or "speech director," who had a little dance step and who recited the following rhyme:

> *Here we stand before your door,*
> *As we stood the year before;*
> *Give us whiskey; give us gin,*
> *Open the door and let us in.*

In Philadelphia the tradition continues and the Philadelphia Mummers Association holds a parade each New Year's Day with over ten thousand marchers. The Philadelphia Mummers date back to before the Revolution as a continuation of the Old World customs of ushering in the New Year.

The following is the Cherryville New Year Shooters Chant:

> *Good morning to you, sir. We wish you a happy New Year,*
> *Great health, long life, which God may bestow*
> *So long as you stay here below. May He bestow the house you're in,*
> *Where you go out and you go in. Time by moments steals away,*
> *First the hour and then the day. Small the lost days may appear,*
> *But they soon mount up to a year. Thus another year is gone,*
> *And now it is no more of our own, but if it brings our promises good*
> *As the year before the flood, but let none of us forget*
> *It has left us much in debt, a favor from the Lord received*
> *Since which our spirits hath been grieved. Marked by the unerring hand,*
> *Thus in His book our record stands. Who can tell the vast amounts*
> *Placed to each our accounts? But while you owe the debt is large*
> *You may plead a full discharge. But poor and selfish sinners say,*
> *What can you to justice pay? Trembling last for life is past*
> *And into prison you may be cast. Happy is the believing soul.*
> *Christ for you has paid the whole. We have this New Year's morning*
> *Called you by your name, and disturbed you from your rest,*
> *But we hope no harm by the same. As we ask, come tell us your desire,*
> *And if it be your desire, our guns and pistols they shall fire.*
> *Since we hear of no defiance, you shall hear the art of science.*
> *When we pull trigger and powder burns, you shall hear the roaring of our guns;*
> *Oh, daughters of righteousness, we will rise and warm our eyes*
> *And bless our hearts, for the old year's gone and the New Year's come*
> *And for good luck, we'll fire our guns!*

Howell Stroup is shown preparing for the annual New Year Shoot in this December 31, 1956 photograph. *Courtesy Cherryville Historical Museum.*

Arthur P. Hudson, in his article from *The Southern Folklore Journal* in 1947, tells about a similar old Bohemian custom of "shooting the witches away." According to the great encyclopedic authority on German folklore, *Handworterbuch des deutschen Aberglaubens:*[100]

> *On Sylvester's Eve and on New Year's Day, throughout the land, over fields and plains, in the orchards, and on the streets of cities, there is a brisk shooting, with the idea of "shooting the old year out and shooting the new year in" and greeting and complimenting sweethearts and neighbors. Refreshments from the honorees follow as matter of course.*

In Edwin Miller Fogel's *Beliefs and Superstitions of the Pennsylvania Germans,*[101] the custom of shooting into fruit trees on New Year's Eve is recorded in the form of a proverb, *Bem drage net wammerne net Neijor a schist* ("Fruit trees will not bear unless they are wassailed on New Year's Eve").

At one time there were several groups of shooters in the Gaston and Lincoln County area. There were groups at Beaver Dam, Indian Creek and Bethphage. There were also groups in Catawba County and, according to Gary R. Freeze in his book *The Catawbans*, the custom of "Shooting in the New Year" went west with Catawba Valley migrants to Bollinger County, Missouri. The last recorded instance in Catawba County was in 1892 in Drumsville, northeast of Hickory. The assembled young men appointed a "general" and a "preacher" and marched in military style from house to house, accompanied by music. The custom died out in Catawba County after 1900.

One hundred years ago New Year Shootings were more common than most people today would think. According to Major William A. Graham in the *North Carolina Booklet, 1914*, the custom originated in Germany when tenants went to the mansion of the baron or landlord and saluted him as a mark of respect. In other times, the "shootings" apparently ended with a breakfast, when the "Preacher" or "Crier" left the young folk, who then opened a program of prize shooting, drinking and dancing. One version of an ancient chant ends with:

> *Our guns shall either snap or fire*
> *As I hear no objections,*
> *We'll now proceed to your protection.*

If, on account of sickness or some other reason, firing was not desired, the landlord would call out "snap." Major Graham stated that a large attendance at the shooting was considered a good omen for the next wheat crop, "caused by the settling of the powder smoke upon the ground." After the shooting, the landlord was supposed to invite the shooters in and "treat" them.

Returning to Gaston County to experience the pageantry of the New Year Shoot is like a pilgrimage for many who return each year with their families. For people who grew up in the Cherryville area, as I did, the sound of black powder brings nostalgic memories as the first familiar musket booms are heard in the wee hours of the morning echoing down Indian Creek or breaking the silence on Little Beaverdam as the shooters trek across. The sound is said to be clearest in that coldest hour just before dawn; that hour between the edge of night and the break of day, when the darkness rolls away with the smoke of the muskets.

All through New Year's Day, the muskets sound their New Year salute until sunset, and then they fall silent for another year.

Of interest is the following list of homes and businesses visited in 1955 by the Cherryville New Year Shooters:

1955 Schedule of New Year Shooters

Dwight Sweatt	*Jim Carroll*
Mrs. Lee Dellinger	*"Doc" Shull*
D.D. Black	*Rhyne-Houser Mill*
VFW	*Florence Ford*
Ed Chapman	*Ben Black*
Oscar Blackburn	*Carolina Freight*

Violet Carpenter
Guy Beam
Pete Howell
F.L. Beam
Ray Beam
Esper Wright
Thea Beam
Guy Brown
Sam P. Wehunt
Floyd Beam
O. H. Venters
Bush Miller
Roy Taylor
Rush Beam
Zenus Dellinger
Pete Bess
Bud Boyles

Tom Hovis
Carlton Mill
Club Carolina
Arvil Homesley
Sam Sellers
Firestone
Bill Blackwelder
James Homesley
Earl Childers
Nuway Mill
Long's Metal Shop
Emmitt Brown
George Houser
Jesse Vandyke
Charles Hoyle
Jane Lineberger
Carpenter's Funeral Home

New Year Shooters preparing to shoot in the New Year at the Homesley home around 1910. *Courtesy Cherryville Historical Museum.*

The families of Beam, Brown, Carpenter, Homesley, Kester, Lackey, Neil, Pfieffer, Quinn, Self, Sellers, Shull and Stroup are well represented in this circa 1955 picture of the Cherryville New Year Shooters. *Courtesy Cherryville Historical Museum.*

Michael Leonhardt　　　　*Lee Cauble*
John Lee Black　　　　　*Fred Houser*
Ruffin White　　　　　　*Hartman's*

The Lutheran Church in Gaston County

The three earliest Lutheran Churches in Gaston County were Kastner's (Philadelphia), Beaver Dam (Saint Mark's) and Bethel. Philadelphia Lutheran Church is the oldest Lutheran Church west of the Catawba River and the second-oldest church in Gaston County.

Philadelphia Lutheran Church

To follow the history of Philadelphia Lutheran Church, we must go back to eighteenth-century Germany. One of the men who fled Southern Germany in the early eighteenth century was Adam Kastner along with his wife and children. They arrived in Philadelphia in September of 1748 on the ship *Patience*. They stayed a short time in York County, Pennsylvania, and then headed south to the Piedmont of North Carolina, bringing with them the huge German

Adam Kastner, his wife and children came to Philadelphia, Pennsylvania, from Germany on the ship, *Patience*, in September 1748. He brought with him this Kastner (Costner) Family Bible. *Courtesy Gaston County Art and History Museum.*

Bible they had brought from Germany. They established their home on the west bank of the South Fork River, a short distance below the church site near Freytag Shoals.[102] Some time before the end of 1767, Adam Kastner and his neighbors, other German pioneers who had come to North Carolina, met and made plans to establish a church. At first, church services were held in different homes.

The first church building, which was probably made of logs, was near the Old Philadelphia Church Cemetery. Adam Kastner was considered the founder of the church and so the church bore his name. The church was known as Kastner's Church until 1776. At that time the name was changed to Philadelphia Lutheran Church.

Laymen and itinerant ministers served the church until 1785 when Reverend Johann Gottfried Arndt accepted the call to come to the Philadelphia Church area. During Arndt's ministry, a log church was built. The pastors to follow Arndt, who left in 1807, were: Reverend Philip Henkel (1814); Reverend Daniel Moser, who left in 1821; Reverend David Henkel (1821); Reverend Adam Miller (1831); Reverend George Easterly (until 1833); Reverend Jesse Peterson, a native of Gaston County who was called in 1845 and served fifty-two years; Reverend Willis Alexander Deaton (until 1907); Reverend Paul David Risinger; and Reverend Alfred Riley Beck (until 1917).

During the 1916 flood, the water rose in the church to within eighteen inches of the eaves. It was decided at that time to relocate the church to higher ground. A church was built and a new cemetery was started on land given by John Quinn.

A few feet to the south of the Old Beaver Dam Graveyard stood Beaver Dam Church, one of the oldest Lutheran Churches in North Carolina. *Photo by Rita Wehunt-Black.*

Bethel Lutheran Church

Bethel Lutheran Church is located near Pasour's Mountain, at the gap. According to historians Phillip Leonard and Robert C. Carpenter, Reverend Johann Friederich Doubbert, a German, was an early religious influence in the Bethel Church area. He had received a land grant on April 16, 1765, for two hundred acres. He most certainly established a church at the gap of Pasour's Mountain.

Very little is known about the church at the gap of Pasour's Mountain because no records have survived, except for a few entries in pastors' journals. From Bethel Church histories, we learn that the "the first church was built of logs and was located on the west side of the Old Cherryville-Dallas Road on the first knoll north of the gap of Pasour's Mountain." This first church had a cemetery, but it is no longer visible.

Robert C. Carpenter, in the *History of Bethel Evangelical Lutheran Church*, tells about a source he found in the North Carolina State Archives in Raleigh located in the road records. This record mentions the maintenance of roads by citizens where the local courts would require residents to keep roads in good repair. These records are invaluable to genealogists and should not be overlooked when doing research. In the April sessions of 1803, the court

PASOUR

PAYSOUR·PAYSEUR·PASEUR

PIONEER GEORGE PASOUR (BASHORE)
WAS BURIED IN A CHURCH CEMETERY
NEAR HERE, GIVING THIS MOUNTAIN
ITS NAME, THROUGH SON GEORGE
PASOUR, JR. 1764-1851 AND WIFE
HANNAH HOYLE, SPRANG MANY
DESCENDANTS.

1967

Thomas J. Marino wrote about the Pasour, Paysour, Payseur, Paseur, Bosshaar family in his 1992 book entitled *Pasour, Paysour, Payseur, Paseur, Together...at Last.* This monument is located on the Dallas-Cherryville Highway. *Photo by Rita Wehunt-Black.*

Bethel Lutheran Church (1893) is a Designated Gaston County Historic Property. *Photo by Rita Wehunt-Black.*

appointed overseers to a road that ran from Lincolnton to the South Carolina line. The first part of the road ran from Lincolnton to Long Shoals. The second part of the road ran from "long Shoal to little mountain-meetinghouse." The overseer for this "out of repair" section of road was John Carpenter. The third leg of the road ran "from little mountain-meetinghouse to Jno. Whitsides"; its overseer was John Hoyle.

During Reverend Philip Henkel's ministry in 1814, the Bethel congregation recorded its first land deed. The land was located on the south side of the Shoal Branch of Long Creek (Lincoln County Land Deeds) and contained a spring. The congregation called the church the Long Creek Congregation.

On Sunday, June 11, 1814, David Henkel preached at the church and noted it as "Longcreek." David Henkel would remain for fifteen years serving Bethel and Beaver Dam. Kiser writes that from 1820 until 1835 there was no regular minister, and some members joined Beaver Dam Lutheran and the Methodists. On June 2, 1827, Reverend David Henkel recorded his last visit to "Longcreek."

Reverend Johann Gottfried Arndt was in the area beginning in 1776 as a Lutheran itinerant preacher. Sometime around 1790, Reverend Arndt began preaching at "the church at the mountain." Henkel's Diary (1818) mentions a church that was at Pasour's Mountain that burned and was never rebuilt. From Robert Carpenter's research, it appears that the church could have been rebuilt on the site since road records prove that a church building existed in 1803.

A notation on back of this old photograph reads, "Dallas Girls Academy Graduating Class. First row 5th from left Margaret Lucy Stroup, wife of Dr. A.W. Howell." *Courtesy Cherryville Historical Museum.*

At Dallas, the Lutheran Synod and Reverend M.L. Little, pastor at Antioch Lutheran Church, helped establish a high school in the 1880s that developed into Gaston College for Girls. Professor S.A. Wolf was principal. *Courtesy Lutheran Synod of North Carolina.*

Saint Mark's Lutheran Church

Saint Mark's Lutheran Church is located four miles from Cherryville. The original location, when it was called Beaver Dam Church, was about a mile east of the present location on Beaver Dam Creek. It was in that location that the first record of the church was written by Reverend Gottfried Arndt, whose journal states that he held services of Communion there in 1786. The congregation applied for, and later received, a land grant for fifty acres on March 2, 1790.

In 1801, John Teeter Beam built the congregation a new "Meeting House" on his property. About two years later, the congregation sold the fifty acres from the land grant and did not own land again until 1819. On March 6, 1819, the tract of land where the church had been meeting was purchased. This included the "Meeting House and the grave yard." The old constitution, drawn up by Reverend David Henkel, was written in both English and German in May 1823.

It is believed that Reverend Paul Henkel preached there in the early days of his ministry, and the Reverend David Henkel served this congregation regularly from 1814 until 1830. It was around this time that the schism in the Lutheran Church in America occurred, and the subsequent formation of the Tennessee Synod in 1819–20. The two ministers who became the leaders in the division were Reverend Gottlieb Schober, on the part of the North Carolina Synod, and Reverend David Henkel, on the part of the withdrawing party, which afterwards formed the Tennessee Synod.[103]

Saint Mark's Lutheran Church, Cherryville, North Carolina. The first written record of its existence appears in a pastor's journal in 1786, but the congregation could have been in existence as early as 1760 at Beaver Dam. *Photo by Rita Wehunt-Black.*

In May of 1856, it was decided to build a new church about a mile west of the old one, and land was secured at the intersection of what would become Saint Mark's Church Road and Sunbeam Farm Road, Cherryville, North Carolina. The first structure was a white frame building, thirty-five by forty-five feet, and was dedicated on May 8, 1858. It was then that the name was changed from Beaver Dam to Saint Mark's Lutheran Church. The pastor at that time was Reverend J.R. Peterson. In 1924, the sanctuary was expanded, remodeled and brick veneered under the leadership of Reverend C.O. Lippard. On August 28, 1927, the new building was dedicated under Pastor F.M. Speagle.

In the 1950s, Saint John's Lutheran Church in Cherryville removed the stained-glass windows and the lighting fixtures in preparation for building a new church building. They were installed at Saint Mark's.

At one time Saint Mark's was in a multiple-church parish that included Bethpage, Saint Paul's Lutheran and Bethel. Bethpage and Saint Paul's are located in Lincoln County.

Lutheran pastor Luther L. Lohr served at Antioch Lutheran Church, Saint Mark's Lutheran, Saint John's Lutheran in Cherryville, Lutheran Chapel in Gastonia and many other churches in North Carolina. *Courtesy Lutheran Synod of North Carolina.*

ANSWER

TO

Mr. JOSEPH MOORE, THE METHODIST;

WITH A FEW

FRAGMENTS ON THE DOCTRINE

OF

JUSTIFICATION.

By DAVID HENKEL,
Pastor of the Evangelic Lutheran Church, residing in Lincoln county, N.C.

NEW MARKET, VA.

PRINTED IN S. HENKEL'S OFFICE, BY S. G. HENKEL.
1825.

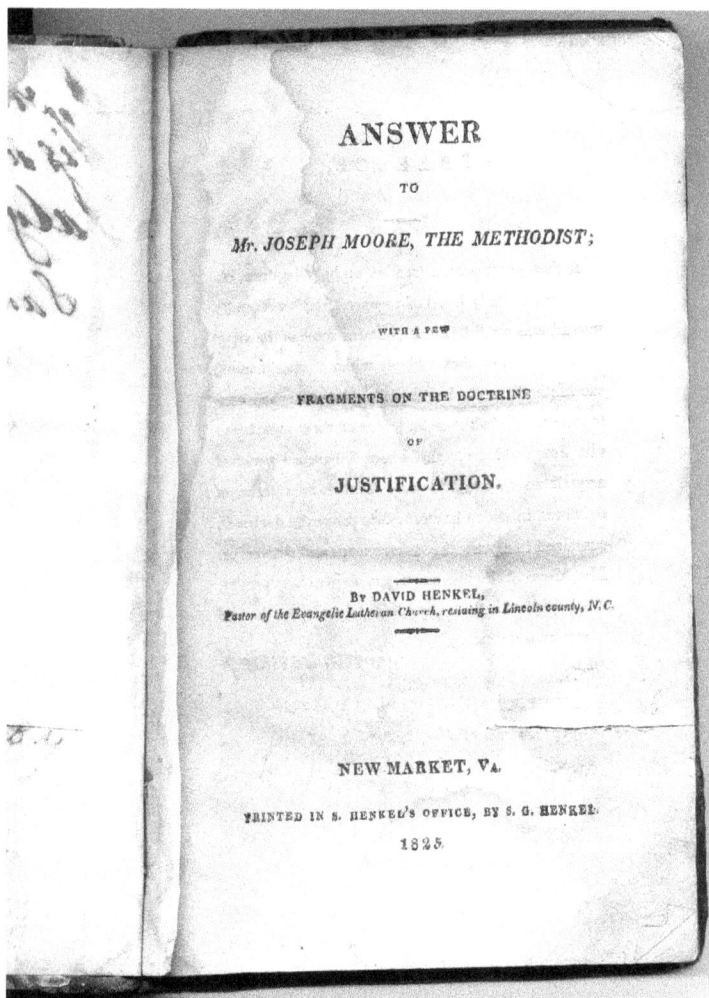

Lutheran pastor David Henkel's book, *Answer to Mr. Moore, the Methodist; With a Few Fragments on the Doctrine of Justification*, belonged to John Wehunt (1798–1886) and has been in the Wehunt Family since 1825. *Courtesy of Rita Wehunt-Black and family.*

Over the years Saint Mark's Lutheran Church and the proclamation of the Gospel have caused the birth of other congregations, such as Saint John's Lutheran Church in Cherryville, Saint Luke's Lutheran Church in Kings Mountain and Mount Hebron Lutheran Church in Henry River.

CHAPTER 7

The Early Mills

Child Labor and Mill Strikes

Lewis Hine (1874–1940) was born in Oshkosh, Wisconsin. He was a humanist whose photography helped to educate the public about the problem of child labor right after the turn of the century. While at New York University's School of Education, he began his photography that would make him famous.

In 1907 Hine was given a full-time assignment with the National Child Labor Committee in which he was to photograph the conditions of child labor. He photographed child labor in many different settings. His photos include children working in factories, mills, tenements and street trade. In 1908–1912, he traveled south and photographed child labor in cotton mills in North Carolina, including Gaston County. These powerful and unforgettable images are housed at the Library of Congress in Washington, D.C.

The South experienced a truly remarkable period in labor history between 1929 and 1934. Just when unions had virtually given up on organizing the South, Southern textile workers mobilized and took it upon themselves to address years of low wages, grievances about mill owner control and coercion, the new principles of scientific management and the "stretch-out."

The "stretch-out" was the workers' evocative term for the process of reducing the labor force by ensuring that each worker was as efficient as possible. This practice required more work in the same time period without raising pay and often reducing pay.[104] Hundreds of thousands of workers walked off the job in the South. Mill owners were caught off guard in 1929 when about two thousand millworkers in Gastonia walked out, making demands concerning pay and working conditions. Strikes followed in Bessemer City, Charlotte, Pineville and Marion.[105]

Despite the defeats at Gastonia and Marion, the 1929 strikes would help lead the way for later millworkers throughout the state. In Gastonia, the organization that came in took the form of the Communist-led National Textile Workers Union, while in Marion workers recruited in the AFL's United Textile Workers.[106] Gastonia had the largest mill in the South, the Loray Mill, and this was the main focus of the union. During a skirmish on June 7, 1929,

This picture appeared on the front of a report by the National Child Labor Committee around 1912. The child was from Gaston County, North Carolina. *Courtesy Library of Congress Photo Collection, NCLC, Lewis Hine.*

Doffers at Cherryville Manufacturing Company in Cherryville, North Carolina, in November of 1908. *Courtesy Library of Congress Photo Collection, NCLC, Lewis Hine #263.*

Noontime at the Vivian Cotton Mills, Cherryville, North Carolina. In their 1908 notes, the Department of Labor considered this a better-class mill, well ventilated and lighted. *Courtesy Library of Congress Photo Collection, NCLC, Lewis Hine #0268.*

This photograph was taken during the noon hour, October 23, 1912, at the Loray Mills, Gastonia, North Carolina. After the picture was taken, the boys went back to work in the mill. *Courtesy Library of Congress Photo Collection, NCLC, Lewis W. Hine #3081. Ancestry.com.*

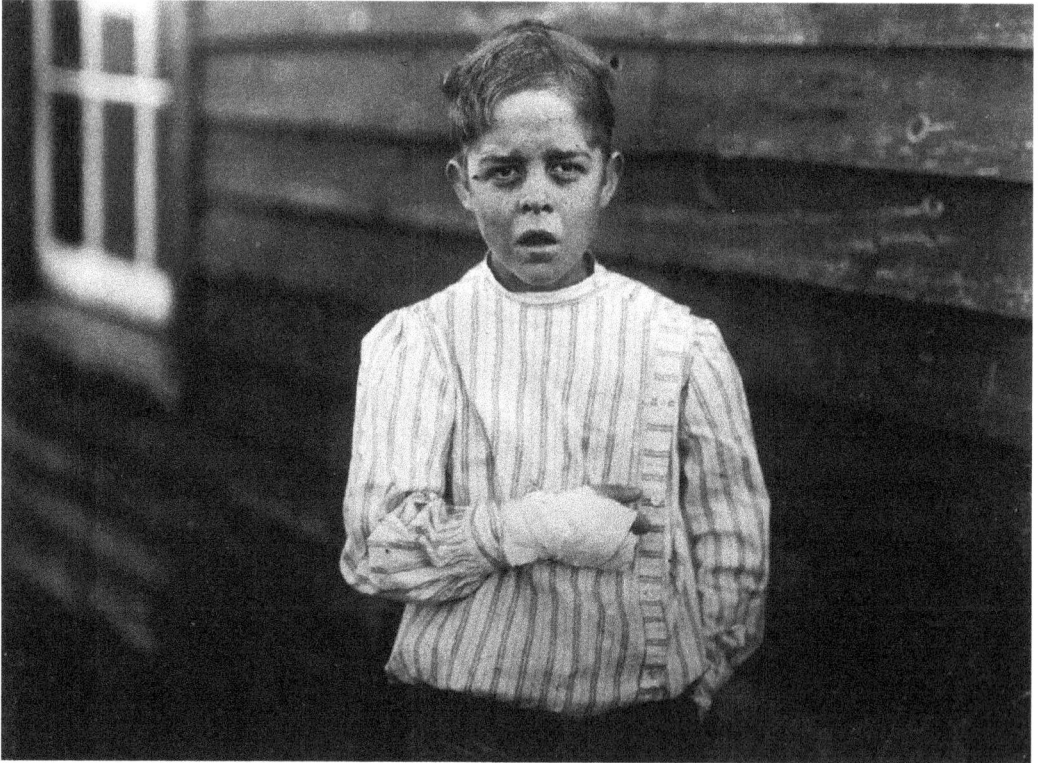

Above: The employment of children in mills was widespread around the turn of the century. It could be a dangerous place for children. This boy from Bessemer City lost two of his fingers. *Courtesy Library of Congress Photo Collection, NCLC, Lewis Hine.*

Left: Strikers at the Loray Mill were often evicted and had to move out of their mill houses into tent villages where they faced more hardship. *Courtesy North Carolina Division of Archives and History.*

Quitting time at Trenton Mill, Gastonia, North Carolina, on a Saturday in 1908. *From left*: Tom Jenkins, Walter Jenkins and John Glover, ages thirteen to sixteen. *Courtesy Library of Congress Photo Collection, NCLC, Lewis Hine #0243. Ancestry.com.*

Young doffers in Cherryville Manufacturing Company in November 1908. *Courtesy Library of Congress Photo Collection, NCLC, Lewis Hine, #0263.Ancestry.com.*

between strikers at union headquarters and the tent village and deputies, the Gastonia Chief of Police Orville F. Aderholt was shot and killed.

A massive rally was planned for September 14, 1929, near the Loray Mill. Workers from neighboring towns would be included in the rally. An armed mob responded by blocking the road, targeting the truck that carried Ella May Wiggins and she was shot and killed.[107] Her funeral was held in Bessemer City by striking workers, and that is where she was buried. Ella May Wiggins had been born to an itinerant logging family in the mountains of North Carolina in 1900. She married and followed a labor recruiter to the Piedmont in the 1920s. By the time of the Gastonia strike, she had given birth to nine children. Her husband had deserted her and four of her children had died. She supported her family by working in the American Mill at Bessemer City. She made nine dollars a week.

The songs of Ella May Wiggins encouraged solidarity among workers during the Gastonia Mill Strike. Some of her songs were written from her personal hardships, such as "Mill Mother's Lament." After her death, her music remained popular and had an influence on later musicians.[108] Some of the lyrics from "Mill Mother's Lament" follow:

We leave our home in the morning,
We kiss our children goodbye,
While we slave for the bosses
Our children scream and cry.

And when we draw our money
Our grocery bills to pay,
Not a cent to spend for clothing,
Not a cent to lay away.

And on that very evening,
Our little son will say:
"I need some shoes, dear mother,
And so does sister May."

How it grieves the heart of a mother,
You every one must know.
But we can't buy for our children,
Our wages are too low.

The workers' grievances, solidarity and frustrations were reflected in Ella May Wiggins's ballads and her songs spread throughout the region, helped by radio and other "cotton mill musicians."

Many books have been written on the Loray Mill strike, including *Gastonia 1929: The Story of the Loray Mill Strike* by John Salmond and *The Thirteenth Juror* by Robert Williams. A development project for the old Loray Mill, sometimes called the Firestone Mill, and a state marker are in the works.

Ella May Wiggins, killed September 14, 1929, during the Loray Mill strike of 1929, is buried in the Bessemer City Memorial Cemetery. *Photo by Rita Wehunt-Black.*

Ella May Wiggins and a friend in 1929. *Courtesy of UPI/Bettmann Newsphotos.*

CHAPTER 8

It Takes a (Mill) Village

At the turn of the century in Gaston County most millworkers lived in villages and mill houses owned by the mill owners. If several mills were located in a village or town, the neighborhoods were called "mill hills" by the workers who lived there. Sometimes the mill established the contours of everyday existence.[109] Gaston County mill villages were born out of necessity, since most early mills were built in the country along riverbanks, and the mill owners had little choice but to provide housing for their workers.

At first, a typical village consisted of the mill, a superintendent's house, a cluster of single-family dwellings, one or more frame churches, a company store, a one-room schoolhouse, perhaps the dwelling of a doctor or midwife and sometimes a local undertaker. Within the village men and women lived out their lives; thus, the expression that was often heard in the village, "From Cradle to the Grave." People in the village had gardens and barns for their animals, and they helped their neighbors during hard times just as they had done in rural settings. Some millworkers created their own alternative churches and held emotional revivals to the dismay of the mill owners.[110] Revivals also dramatized the social and psychological distance between the mill owners and the millworkers. Liston Pope writes in *Millhands and Preachers* that the new sect churches in Gastonia drew their entire membership from among millworkers.[111]

The transformation from rural village to mill village, farmers-turned-mill hands, took place all over Gaston County. Old habits and customs were hard to leave behind and these customs blended in the new mill villages. When Southern farmers left the land and took a cotton mill job, they called it "Public work."[112] For an in-depth social history of the mill village, the following are notable historical works, *Like a Family: The Making of a Southern Cotton Mill World* by Jacquelyn Dowd Hall, James Leloudis, Robert Korstad, Mary Murphy, Lu Ann Jones and Christopher B. Daly; and *The Voice of Southern Labor: Radio, Music, and Textile Strikes, 1929–1934* by Vincent J. Roscigno and William F. Danaher.

Things began to change for millworkers after the 1930s. Safety issues were looked at; some mills provided summer camps, clubhouses with swimming pools and nurses. There were Christmas bonuses and gifts of food and other items. The mills took more of a human

This very pretty young girl had been working two years as a spinner in the Vivian Cotton Mill when this picture was taken in 1908 in Cherryville, North Carolina. *Courtesy Library of Congress Photo Collection, NCLC, Lewis W. Hine #0271.*

interest in the workers. Mill owners donated money for churches, schools, colleges, paid "doctor bills" and offered many other things—there were baseball teams, social workers, recreational directors and clubs. Those who grew up in the 1940s and '50s, and even some who grew up in earlier times, have fond memories of growing up in the mill villages, and they talk as if it was one very large extended family where everybody on the "hill" looked after one another.

Some workers refused to participate in company-sponsored activities, thinking that they were intended to keep them docile and loyal, and "company welfare work" sometimes failed to produce dramatic results because workers drew on the strengths of their own communities to avoid dependence on their employers.[113]

Music at the Bandstand

Music has always been a part of human history and Gaston County had its share of music. Most small villages and towns had a bandstand and "Town Band." Some families had phonographs, but most relied on their own means for making music.

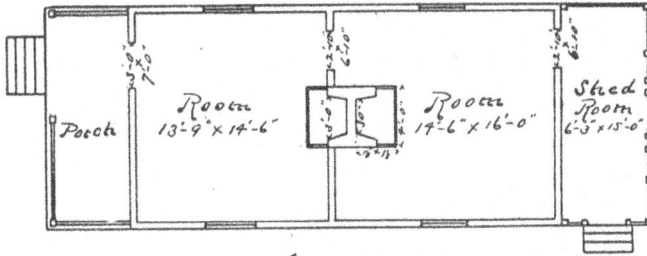

Floor Plan

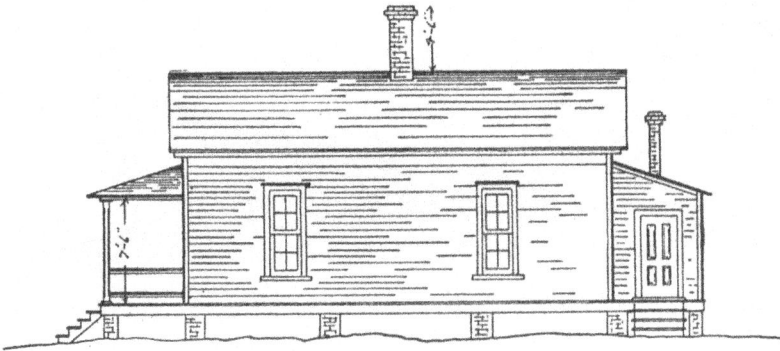

Side Elevation

Front Elevation

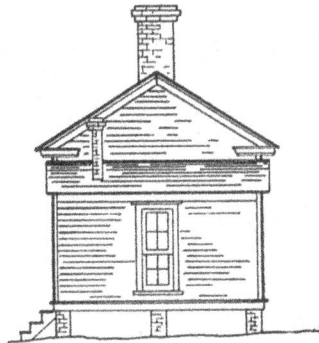

Rear Elevation

Blueprints for a two-room mill house at a cost of $250 to build. This style was known as a "shotgun house." *Courtesy Cherryville Historical Museum.*

An aerial view of Howell Manufacturing and "mill village" in Cherryville; note the clubhouse. *Courtesy Cherryville Historical Museum.*

Cherryville's Howell Manufacturing Company employees, 1938.

An unnamed woman working at a beam warper in a textile mill in Cherryville, North Carolina, in November of 1908. *Courtesy Library of Congress Photo Collection, NCLC, Lewis W. Hine #0304.*

This unidentified young girl was a spinner at the Cherryville Manufacturing Company in Cherryville, North Carolina. The picture was taken in 1908. *Courtesy Library of Congress Photo Collection, NCLC, Lewis W. Hine #0309.*

The inside of a typical tabernacle, such as those built in Gaston County in the early 1900s. *Courtesy Rita Wehunt-Black.*

Gastonia's first orchestra was organized in 1910 by Lillian Atkins Michael, who was an accomplished musician herself. Some of the members of this early orchestra were Fred D. Barkly, Ken Todd, Fred Stowe and Hunter Morrow. Some of the songs popular in Gaston County around 1910 were "Oh, You Beautiful Doll," "Alexander Ragtime Band" and "Temptation Rag." For several summers this orchestra played at Linwood College, located below Crowders Mountain. When Tom Browning, the evangelist, was in Gastonia, the Main Street Methodist Church, later to become the First United Methodist Church, erected a tabernacle where part of the orchestra played every night for three weeks.

One of the best-known bands in the county was from High Shoals. The band performed in the parks on the meadow by the river in High Shoals. At one time, High Shoals was a favorite picnic place for groups from Gastonia and other towns in the county. There was a sunken garden below the bridge and a broad expanse of rock floor just above the dam. These areas were equipped with picnic tables, swings, merry-go-round and athletic fields.[114]

The Mount Holly town band was also a popular and well-known band, as was the McAdenville Brass Band in the late 1890s and into the early 1900s. The Mount Holly Band,

Carlton Yarn Mill Band, 1925–26. *Front*: Streeter Frye, Ed Frye and Monroe Randall. *Second row*: Lewis Sneed, Noah Mauney, Kelly Huss, Caldwell Farnsworth and Guy Sneed. *Third row*: Howard Allran, Raymond Randall, Russell Frye, Floyd L. Mauney and Bill Harmon Rufus Mauney. *Courtesy Cherryville Museum.*

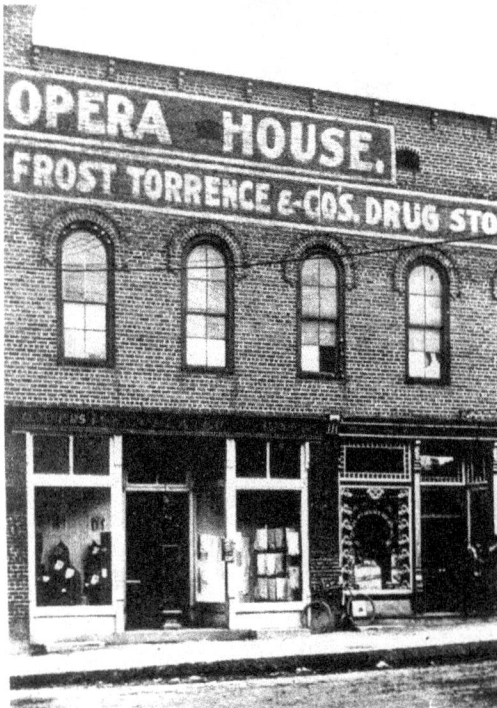

Above: The Cherryville Town Band, 1904, played for special events. Pictured are David Rudisill, Marcus Mauney, Lee McGinnis, John Moss, Vitchel Stroup, Bishop Roberts, Ed Frye, Buford Moss, L.H.J. Houser, Frank Putnam, Stephen Stroup, J.B. Houser and Evon Houser. *Courtesy Cherryville Museum.*

Left: The Frost Torrence Building in Gastonia housed the community Opera House on the second floor. The first floor was a drugstore. *Courtesy Gaston County Museum of Art and History.*

An unidentified Gaston County band is shown in this picture from the 1920s. *Courtesy Cherryville Historical Museum.*

known as the Euterpean Band and founded by Washington R. Holland, was invited to play at the inauguration of President William McKinley in 1897.[115] Later, some of the mills had "mill bands" and choirs. The church choirs and school choirs also sang at many functions. Later, high schools would have marching bands.

Early Southern musicians and "radio musicians" were strongly affected by their work in the cotton mills. "The Brierhoppers" of Gastonia began their careers while working in the mills in Gastonia in the 1930s. David McCarn, a native of Gastonia, who recorded "Cotton Mill Colic," had also worked in a mill. "Cotton Mill Colic" sold out quickly in Gastonia and became popular throughout the Southern textile belt.[116] Some musicians continued to work in the mills between music jobs.[117] In Marion, North Carolina, musician Bill Monroe and others would congregate outside of the mill villages of Marion.

Along with the mill and religion, music had a way of bonding the people together as they sat on the porches in the mill villages.

The Hat Lady

At one time there was a lady milliner, known as "the Hat Lady," living in Gaston County. This was at a time when few ladies left their homes without their hats. The Hat Lady's name was Mary Margaret Litton, but most people called her Maggie; sometimes she preferred Madge.

Maggie Litton was born in South Carolina on November 7, 1861, to George W. Quinn and his wife Genellia Putnam Quinn. Maggie's father, who had moved his family to North Carolina, had at one time been a tailor, but later he was known as the axe handle maker. Maggie and Sanford Litton were married on January 30, 1901, by the Baptist minister, at her mother's home in Cherryville. Her father had died. Maggie did not give her correct age—she was thirty-nine, but said she was thirty. Sanford was twenty-two. Sanford Litton apparently died very early in their marriage, so Maggie was a widow. It is thought that she and Sanford never had children, but there may have been a son.

After the death of her husband, Maggie moved from town to town in Gaston County making hats for a living for the rest of her life. In the U.S. Federal Census for 1910, she showed up in Gastonia, North Carolina, boarding with James E. Steward, a tailor, and his wife, Annie Westen Steward, a dressmaker. Maggie's occupation was listed as a milliner in a store. Again, she knocked more than a few years off of her age and gave it as forty years old; she also stated that she was a widow. Gastonia at that time had several department stores that had milliners working in them. We do not know in which store Maggie worked, but it was probably one of the ones listed in the *Illustrated Handbook of Gastonia, N.C.*, published in 1906 by Joseph H. Separk:

> *John F. Love—Dry Goods, Notions, Millinery, Shoes, Clothing*
> *James F. Yeager—Ladies' Furnishings, Millinery, Manufacturer of Ladies Garments*
> *J.M. Belk Company—Dry Goods, Shoes, Clothing, Millinery*
> *D. Lebovitz—Dry Goods, Shoes, Clothing, Millinery*

Almost a decade later, in 1918, Maggie had left Gastonia and was living in Cherryville, North Carolina, where she operated a hat shop in a small building on First Street, where the Cherryville Ice and Fuel Company would later be located and today is the site of a skate park. A newspaper article from the *Cherryville Eagle*, dated January 4, 1918, stated that her two nieces, Miss Candace Quinn, age twenty-six, and Miss Bertha Quinn, age twenty-two, from Gaffney, South Carolina, were visiting her. These were the daughters of her brother, Sherman "Speed" Quinn, who seemed to move quite frequently between South Carolina and Gaston County, North Carolina, with his large family.

In the *Cherryville Eagle* dated September 25, 1919, Maggie had the following announcement:

> *My new hats have arrived. The prices are reasonable. Come and buy yourself a nice hat and be ready for the fall season. My place of business is still at my old home near the Rail Road. Most Respectfully, Mrs. Maggie Litton.*

Hattie Peeler Self, wife of Dr. L.L. Self of Cherryville, may be wearing one of "The Hat Lady's" hats. *Courtesy Cherryville Historical Museum.*

Maggie was a very friendly and outgoing person and had many friends in Gaston County, especially Mrs. Levi (Etta) Houser. Mrs. Houser and her husband lived in Cherryville where he published the town newspaper, the *Cherryville Eagle*.

There is a very interesting story that has been handed down through oral history by many families in the Cherryville area concerning the Hat Lady. It seems that while living in Cherryville, Maggie decided to order herself a mail-order husband, and he was to arrive on the train from New Jersey with a flower in his lapel. Maggie had sent him a photograph that was perhaps one of her nieces, but was definitely not Maggie herself. When the stranger got off the train in Cherryville wearing a flower in his lapel, as had been agreed upon, he saw only two ladies waiting at the depot. The gentleman from New Jersey looked the two ladies over, then turned and got back on the train and continued south, much to Maggie's dismay.

From her Gaston County death certificate, we learn that Maggie Litton died on February 18, 1927, at the age of sixty-five of a cerebral hemorrhage, after being attended by Dr. A.W. Howell at the boardinghouse where she lived. She was buried in Black's Cemetery in Cherryville, in the county of Gaston that she loved so well. The people of Gaston County must have also loved Maggie Litton, for her memory is alive after so many years.

Daniel Efrid Rhyne

Daniel E. Rhyne was an interesting and colorful individual. He was descended from Jacob Rhyne, who settled on upper Hoyle's Creek around 1794 and fathered eight children.[118] Daniel Efrid Rhyne was born to Moses and Margaret Elizabeth Hoffman Rhyne on February 8, 1852. His father, along with Frederick Hoffman, owned the Hoffman-Rhyne mercantile store at Mount Holly. It was in that store that a meeting was held in 1842 to consider the question of dividing Lincoln County. This meeting resulted in the creation of Gaston County from the southern part of Lincoln County in 1846.[119]

In addition to his interest in gold mines, a tin mine in Lincoln County, his numerous cotton mills and his gifts to Lenoir-Rhyne College, Daniel became the owner of the Piedmont Wagon Manufacturing Company in Hickory, North Carolina, in 1916. The following is part of a brochure printed by the company; the year is uncertain:

> *The South is fortunate in having located at Hickory, North Carolina, a manufacturing establishment of the importance and capacity of the Piedmont Wagon & Manufacturing Company, of which Mr. D.E. Rhyne is the president and sole owner.*
>
> *Mr. Rhyne is well known throughout the South as one of its foremost financiers, a progressive manufacturer and a leader in the textile industry. He is one of the men directly responsible for the rapid growth of industry south of the Mason-Dixon Line. He is a man of recognized constructive ability and a firm believer in the policy of manufacturing only products that meet the rigid demands of highest quality. The quality of PIEDMONT and HICKORY wagons shows that this policy is strictly adhered to.*
>
> *The first PIEDMONT wagon was built in 1877 by G.H. Geitner in a little blacksmith shop, northwest of Hickory, North Carolina. He built this wagon as good as his long experience repairing wagons and studying their construction would permit.*

A Lincolnton newspaper article in November of 1899 announced that he was the first person in North Carolina to own an automobile. Mr. Rhyne never married and died on February 25, 1933. When Daniel Rhyne died, he left a multimillion-dollar estate.[120] He is buried at Lutheran Chapel Church in Gastonia.

Right: Daniel E. Rhyne (1852–1931) was a banker, textile manufacturer, owner of gold and tin mines, owner of a wagon factory and owned the first car in North Carolina. Lenoir-Rhyne College was named for him. *Courtesy Cherryville Historical Museum.*

Below: Gaston County students are among this graduating class at Lenoir College in this undated photograph. Lenoir College would become Lenoir-Rhyne College, named for D.E. Rhyne and W.W. Lenoir. *Courtesy Cherryville Historical Museum.*

MR. D. E. RHYNE
Manufacturer and Financier. Sole Owner of the
PIEDMONT WAGON & MANUFACTURING COMPANY
of Hickory, N. C.

Hunter Huss

Often called the patriarch of Gaston County education, Webb Hunter Huss was born March 5, 1902, in Cherryville, North Carolina. His parents were A. Hoke Huss and Mary Louola Stroup. He married Harriet Temple and they had two sons and two daughters.

Huss started his career in education in 1923 in Cramerton, North Carolina, after graduating from the University of North Carolina. He soon moved from Cramerton to North Belmont. From there he went to Cherryville and was principal of Cherryville High School for seven years. In 1832 he was named superintendent of the Cherryville City Schools.

In 1937 he was called to Gastonia to become superintendent of the Gaston County Schools. He held this position from 1937 until his retirement in 1968. He had spent forty-five years in the field of education in Gaston County. Hunter Huss died in April of 1971.

Dr. W.B. Sugg, president of Gaston College in 1971, was quoted as saying, "He was a great big man who loved people and loved school children and didn't particularly like for people to know it." Huss had talked about a community college in Gaston County as far back as 1940.

Huss was proud of Gaston County and his German heritage, and he was a member of Holy Trinity Lutheran Church in Gastonia. His legacy in Gaston County includes a scholarship fund in his name at Gaston College and, most notably, Hunter Huss High School, which was named for him.

Hunter Huss (far right) with the 1926 Cherryville Football team. *Courtesy Cherryville Historical Museum.*

Carl Augustus Rudisill

Carl Augustus Rudisill established the Carlton Yarn Mills and was one of the foremost textile manufacturers in the South. He pioneered many new fields in the industry. He was known far and wide for his ability to prescribe for a "sick" mill. He was the son of Poly C. and Lavinia Rudisill, and was born in Lincoln County, North Carolina, in 1884. His family moved to Gaston County when he was quite young. Following schooling, his first job was that of a doffer boy in a cotton mill in Cherryville. Young Mr. Rudisill's wages were ten cents a day. Advancing from job to job, he was able to gain firsthand knowledge of all the phases involved in the manufacturing of cotton yarn. While at Lenoir-Rhyne College in Hickory, and at North Carolina State College in Raleigh, he defrayed school expenses by selling fruit trees and enlarging photographs. Because of his technical knowledge and practical training, he advanced rapidly in the textile industry. By 1907, he was superintendent of the Indian Creek Manufacturing Company.

Early in his career, Mr. Rudisill married Verner Dellinger and had a daughter, Margaret, and a son, Ben Richard Rudisill.

Later in his career, Carl Rudisill developed Carlton Yarn Mills into the finest yarn mills in the country. He served in the North Carolina legislature from 1937 until 1941. Carl Rudisill, a loyal and devoted Lutheran, died on September 9, 1979.

Carl A. Rudisill, one of the foremost textile manufacturers of Gaston County, established the Carlton Yarn Mills and pioneered many new fields in the industry. He served in the North Carolina Legislature from 1937 until 1941. *Courtesy Cherryville Historical Museum.*

Our internet culture has devalued paper records. Scrapbooks packed with small-town newspaper clippings, handwritten recipes, old letters and these old Carlton Mill checks are rare Americana. *Courtesy Cherryville Historical Museum.*

George Washington Ragan (1846–1936)

The early members of the Ragan family were among the first settlers of Lincoln County, in the area that later would become Gaston County. In his 1995 book entitled *The Ragans of Gastonia 1790–1995*, Robert A. Ragan says that the family is of Irish extraction and states, "My research leads to the conclusion that the name is 'pure' Irish and probably of Celtic origin." However, family members undoubtedly intermarried with the later arriving Scots in Northern Ireland and became part of that great Scots-Irish exodus from Northern Ireland in the eighteenth century.

George Washington Ragan was born into this family on September 16, 1846, to Daniel Franklin and Harriet Glenn Ragan. Daniel Franklin Ragan was a farmer, served as a magistrate and member of the North Carolina House of Commons from Gaston County in 1846–48 and for sixteen years was chairman of the Gaston County Court.

George Washington Ragan served in the Civil War at age seventeen. After the war, he returned to his father's farm and then worked in the mercantile business for nineteen years. He did not have a formal education, but he was self-educated and went on to become a banking and textile giant in Gastonia and Gaston County.[121] He assisted in 1889 in organizing the First National Bank of Gastonia and was one of the original stockholders and a director of the first

First Lieutenant Ben R. Rudisill, shown here with the Fifth Ferrying Group at Love Field, Texas, served from 1941 until 1946 and was at the controls of many flights to the European theater of operations. *Courtesy Cherryville Historical Museum.*

cotton mill in Gastonia. He also helped Robert A. Caldwell, George A. Gray and others in 1893 in organizing the Trenton Cotton Mills, Gastonia's second cotton mill. At the Arlington Mill, in 1901, he became the first cotton manufacturer in the South to install combers. In 1922 he formed the Ragan Spinning Company.

Mr. Ragan was known for his philanthropies, and was a liberal contributor to Davidson College in North Carolina and Oglethorpe University in Atlanta. He was mayor of Gastonia (1897–1898) and served as a deacon or an elder for fifty years at First Presbyterian Church.

A Young Man's Adventures

Lester Carl Beam, who died in 1976, was one of ten children raised in a log cabin that his father, Peter S. Beam, had built on the banks of Indian Creek, about three miles northeast of Cherryville. The cabin was located near the old homeplace of Peter Beam's immigrant ancestor, Johann Teeter Beam. His mother was Catherine McGinnis. Carl had grown up on adventurous stories told before the open fireplace on winter nights as he sat on the floor of the cabin. The stories that his father told were about the "Indians" for whom the creek was named, the great earthquake and the War Between the States, or the "War of Northern Aggression" as his father called it.

On a knoll above the cabin was a Native American graveyard and Carl played there as a lad while dreaming of a life of adventure. Carl worked in the fields and tramped through the countryside continuing to dream of the adventures he would have when he grew up.

When news arrived in Gaston County of the trouble between the United States and Mexico, Carl knew that this was his chance. Along with three friends, Connolly Helms, Tom Snead and Charlie Watts, Carl sneaked off to Lincolnton, enlisted in the National Guard under Captain Fair's command and found himself in Troop A cavalry. The year would have been 1916 and Carl would have been around nineteen years old. Soon afterwards they were shipped out to El Paso, Texas, on the Mexican border with the armed expedition forces to Mexico to quell raids initiated by the prominent Mexican leader Poncho Villa into the United States.

In command at Camp Cotton was General John J. "Blackjack" Pershing. It was rumored, though untrue, that his wife and children had been killed by Poncho Villa.

Carl never got to see Poncho Villa, but he related the following story to a newspaper reporter in the 1970s about an adventure in a Mexican village. As he was walking back from the village to camp, he heard Charlie Watts's voice coming from one of the adobe huts. Charlie was yelling for help. "I ran back, but the Mexicans had Charlie pinned against a wall and had thirty-eight pistols to his head," Carl recalled.

> *I didn't know what else to do, so I dived over a table and knocked the whole crowd to the floor. Then I slung Charlie over my shoulder and hot footed it out of the hut and across a field. When we came to a four stranded barbed wire fence, I threw Charlie down, and we jumped over and headed across the prairie back to Camp Cotton with the Mexicans close behind. How close behind we didn't know, because we never looked back!*
>
> *Charlie and I came home about a year later without ever really having been involved in major battles. But I kinda think what we had gone through in Mexico was enough. It must have been for Charlie, because he came home and became a barber and stayed in Cherryville the rest of his life.*

Carl recounted some of his experiences and thumbnail sketches of his ancestors in a small book entitled *A History of John Teeter Beam's Generations*. Carl also had a dream of building a tourist attraction in Gaston County similar to Tweetsie Railroad at Blowing Rock, North Carolina, and at the age of seventy he was promoting this idea to others.

Cherry Lane

Elizabeth Black, the wife of Stephen Black (1800–1886), is given credit for giving Cherryville its unique name, and for the start of the cherry trees. Today a Cherry Blossom Festival is held in the town each spring. Mary Frances Mauney, who helped organize the first garden

Raised on Indian Creek, Lester Carl Beam, son of Peter Beam, arrived in El Paso, Texas, on the Mexican border in 1916. *Courtesy Cherryville Historical Museum.*

club (called the Village Garden Club), told many times the old story about the trees, and it was retold and retold again, as it is retold here.

Cherry trees grew in the panhandle section of Gaston County long before Cherryville came into being.[122] One of the old stories says that the town of Cherryville received its name from a lane leading into the little village, which was first known as White Pine. On each side of this lane grew Red Heart cherry trees. Along the lane was a split-rail fence of rails cut from oak and chestnut trees and laid out in a split-rail, zigzag fashion on both sides of the lane. Elizabeth Black planted Red Heart cherry trees in each corner of the rail fence. When the cherries were ripe each year, travelers would stop and feast on the cherries before entering the village. People passing through the village began to speak of the little settlement as "Cherry Lane."

This tale goes on to say that Ephraim Black (1767–1843), who had the first post office, was the first to use the name Cherryville.

Another story, also written by Mary Frances Mauney, is that a group of civil engineers surveying for the railroad, which was to come through the village, were so impressed by the beautiful cherry trees Mrs. Black had set out along the lane that they gave the community the name of Cherryville.

W.T. Robinson related this version of the story: Stephen Black and Elizabeth Brown were married in 1821 and built their home on the Old Post Road leading into town. Stephen and his wife began transplanting cherry trees from the back of their house to corners of the rail fence that ran along the Old Post Road. When the trees began to bloom, others in the area wanted to plant trees along the fence. Soon the road bordered with cherry trees became known as Cherry Lane.

There were many trees by 1862 when the Wilmington, Charlotte & Rutherford Railroad reached the small town of White Pine.[123] Elizabeth Black, sometimes called "Aunt Lizzie," told her grandchildren that a civil engineer, who had supervised the construction of the railroad bed and the first depot, suggested that the name of White Pine be changed to Cherryville. The new name was given to the post office on November 2, 1865, three years after the railroad reached the town.[124]

Reverend C.A. Linn put his own spin on the old tale in 1926 when he wrote that the cherry trees came about because Elizabeth Black had just made a pie, had a pan full of cherry seeds and threw them in an untilled spot behind the garden. Upon the spot where Elizabeth had slung the seeds, cherry trees sprouted, and later Stephen, her husband, transplanted them to the rail fence.

High Sheriff, "The Rurals" and "The Law" in Gaston County

The first lawmen in Gaston were probably the regulators in the 1700s. After Dallas became the county seat of Gaston County, there were twelve sheriffs before the county seat was moved to Gastonia.

The first sheriff after the county seat was moved to Gastonia was Benjamin Morris, who served until 1850. Next came Lawson A. Mason and Paul Froneberger, who was replaced by James F. White in 1860; followed by G.W. McGee, Robert D. Rhyne and R.A. White. In 1891, M.H. Shuford was elected and served until A.K. Loftin took his place.

Serving for four years, starting in 1898, was W.T. Love. He was replaced in 1901 by C.B. Armstrong, also known as Colonel Armstrong. C.B. Armstrong later served as mayor of Gastonia and would become a mill owner in Gaston County.

Wilkie A. McGinnis was replaced by Clyde Robinson in 1935. Sheriff Robinson served as sheriff of Gaston County for twelve years until 1947. Robinson was replaced in 1947 by Hoyle T. Efird.

Sheriff Efird was defeated by Dwight Luther Beam, who served for the next twenty years as sheriff of Gaston County. C.F. Waldrop, a Republican, defeated Beam in 1975.

While Beam was sheriff, the county commissioners created the Gaston County Rural Police in July of 1957, mainly to stamp out moonshiners. The "Rurals," whose patrol cars were originally orange and black, were responsible for criminal police work while the sheriff's office retained the jail and other responsibilities.

Right: Many towns in the early 1900s had a sheriff instead of a police chief. Sheriff Sam Mauney was the sheriff of Cherryville in 1915. He is pictured here with billy club, gun and badge all in plain view. *Courtesy Cherryville Historical Museum.*

Below: The Improved Order of the Red Man was a very popular fraternal order in Gaston County at the end of the nineteenth and beginning of the twentieth centuries. This photograph shows the Dallas Yamassee Tribe #134. *Courtesy Gaston County Museum.*

Above: Suez Temple #73 holds a convention in Cherryville in 1923. The vaudeville, featuring Carlos, is in town, the town band is ready for the parade and Hendricks-Harrelson Furniture and Undertakers are open for business. *Courtesy Cherryville Museum.*

Left: The identities of these two adorable Gaston County children is unknown. *Courtesy Cherryville Historical Museum Family Photographs Collection.*

CHAPTER 9

Towns and Communities in Gaston County

There are fifteen incorporated towns in Gaston County, with Gastonia being the largest in size and Dellview the smallest. There are also many small communities. Among them are Crowders, Sunnyside, Tryon, Lucia, Alexis, Hardin, Boogertown, Hickory Grove, the Highland Community in Gastonia, North Belmont and South Gastonia. All the towns are unique and retain their own character in spite of the fact that all are considered "mill towns."

Dallas

When Gaston County was formed from Lincoln County in 1846, it was stated that the county seat was to be "no more than two miles from Long Creek Baptist Church," one of the first Baptist churches in North Carolina. It was located about one mile east of the present Dallas Town Square. Dallas was chosen for the name of the county seat to honor the United States vice president at that time, George Miffin Dallas.

Seventy-five acres were purchased from Jesse Holland for fifty dollars as a site for the planned town and community. There would be a "Public Square" for the courthouse, a jail, lots for building churches, and lots for businesses and private homes. The money received from the sale of private lots would be used to construct the Greek revival–style courthouse, built in 1848, and the jail.

The lots around the square would later contain the Hoffman Hotel, which was built in 1852 by Daniel Hoffman, the Rhyne Store, built in 1850 by Moses Moore, and the jail at 108 East Trade Street in 1847. The Setzer Building located on West Trade Street was built in the 1870s and constructed with two retail stores on the first floor and living quarters on the second floor.

The oldest known residence is located at 113–115 North Holland Street, and built by Dr. J.F. Smyre in 1850. It was later sold in 1851 to Eli Pasour, the first mayor of Dallas. One of the first private homes was the Robert Lewis House at 100 North Holland Street. It was built in 1852 for John Roberts, who served as the first clerk of court for the county.

The Gaston County Museum of Art and History is located in the Hoffman Hotel, 131 West Main Street, Dallas. It was built in 1852 by Daniel Hoffman. The Daniel Stowe Carriage House is out back. *Photo by Rita Wehunt-Black.*

When the polls closed on August 5, 1909, and the count was completed, Gastonia was named the new county seat of Gaston County by a vote of 2,965 to 2,326.[125] The transfer of the courts, jail, offices and records was set for 1911. Gastonia grew rapidly, but Dallas, at times, seemed in a time warp. The town grew, but retained and cherished its old buildings and its history. And that's a good thing!

Gastonia

In the 1890s, people from miles around were drawn to Gastonia by a spring inside the city limits that was thought to have curative powers. The spring was owned by Dr. W.H. Hoffman, a dentist. It claimed therapeutic benefits comparable to those of Vichy Springs in France.[126] Gastonia became the county's largest town in 1890 with a population of 1,033 people, followed by Mount Holly.

Gastonia was incorporated on January 26, 1877, but would not become the county seat until 1910. Until the arrival of the railroad, it was mostly farmland and forests. Near the town center was the farm of John Craig. Other large landowners were Holland, Davis,

Right: William (Bill) C. Friday, of Dallas, born July 13, 1920, was president of the University of North Carolina from 1956–1986. *Courtesy Cherryville Historical Museum.*

Below: Private First Class Henry T. Johnson (left) of Dallas, North Carolina, and other men of the First Infantry Division, U.S. Army, relax and rest in Germany during World War II. *Courtesy U.S. Army Signal Corps.*

The Old Gaston County Courthouse was completed in 1911. It was designed by the Washington, D.C. firm of Milburn & Heister when the decision was made to move the county seat from Dallas to Gastonia. *Photo by Rita Wehunt-Black*

Rhyne, Wilson and Bradley. The town grew slowly at first. By 1885 there were 485 citizens in the city limits of Gastonia. By 1896, Gastonia's population had grown to 3,000 people.

The first cotton mill was built in Gastonia in 1887. It was called the Gastonia Cotton Manufacturing Company and was established by R.C.G. Love, George A. Gray, J.D. Moore, John Craig and others. In 1893, Mr. George W. Ragan and Mr. George Alexander Gray founded Gastonia's second textile mill called the Trenton Cotton Mills, Inc. Around 1897 George W. Gray and John T. Love founded the Avon Mill.

In 1900–1901,[127] Gray and Love organized and built the Loray Mill (a combination of their names). At the time it was built, it was the largest mill under one roof in the nation. In 1929 the Loray Mill would be the site of the 1929 labor strike. This infamous strike would make Gastonia known all over the United States.

The 1900 census for Gaston County would show Gastonia with a booming population of forty-six hundred citizens. Within the next twelve years, seven mills would be established in Gastonia.

The first hospital in the county was a two-story structure on Airline Avenue built around 1906. This hospital moved to Main Avenue and operated there until around 1924 when it moved to Highland Street, where it later became Gaston Memorial Hospital. Gaston Memorial Hospital operated until 1973 when a new facility was built off Cox Road. The

Right: Built in 1922 by architect Hugh White, Gastonia High School was later renamed Ashley High. The Gothic-style building had a swimming pool and pipe organ. Ashley merged with Holbrook High forming Ashbrook High in 1970. *Photo by Rita Wehunt-Black.*

Below: World War I soldiers from Gaston County assemble on May 28, 1918, at the Gastonia Post Office before leaving for Europe. Built in the early 1900s, the post office was replaced with the present-day post office in 1935. *Courtesy Cherryville Historical Museum.*

Four distinguished Gaston County men pose for this 1949 photograph. They are Governor R. Gregg Cherry, W. Blaine Beam, John L. (Buck) Fraley and State Representative Basil L. Whitener. *Courtesy Cherryville Historical Museum.*

Garrison General Hospital began behind the old Armington Hotel, run by Dr. David Garrison, Dr. James Blair and Dr. H.R. McConnell, with Dr. H.F. Glenn, Dr. L.N. Patrick and others.[128]

Modern Gastonia is a wonderful place to live. Gastonia's "Sister City" is Gotha, Germany. For over ten years, student ambassadors have visited Gotha, Germany, in the spring. They stay with host families while learning about Gotha.

On the National Register of Historic Places in Gastonia are the Old Gaston County Courthouse, Gastonia High School, Robinson-Gardner Building, Loray Mill & Village, Gastonia Downtown Historic District and the York-Chester Historic District.

McAdenville

McAdenville overlooks the South Fork River. The land where present-day McAdenville is located was once owned by James Henderson, and the shoals on the river were known as Henderson Shoals. When Henderson died, he was buried on a hill overlooking the South

The Lutheran Chapel Church Cemetery on New Hope Road in Gastonia. Caleb J. Lineberger (1818–1914) and wife Fannie are among the noted citizens buried here. *Photo by Rita Wehunt-Black.*

Gastonia's Oakland High School faculty in 1899. Oakland High School was constructed in the late 1800s, and became the first public school in Gastonia. *Courtesy of Gaston County Museum of Art and History.*

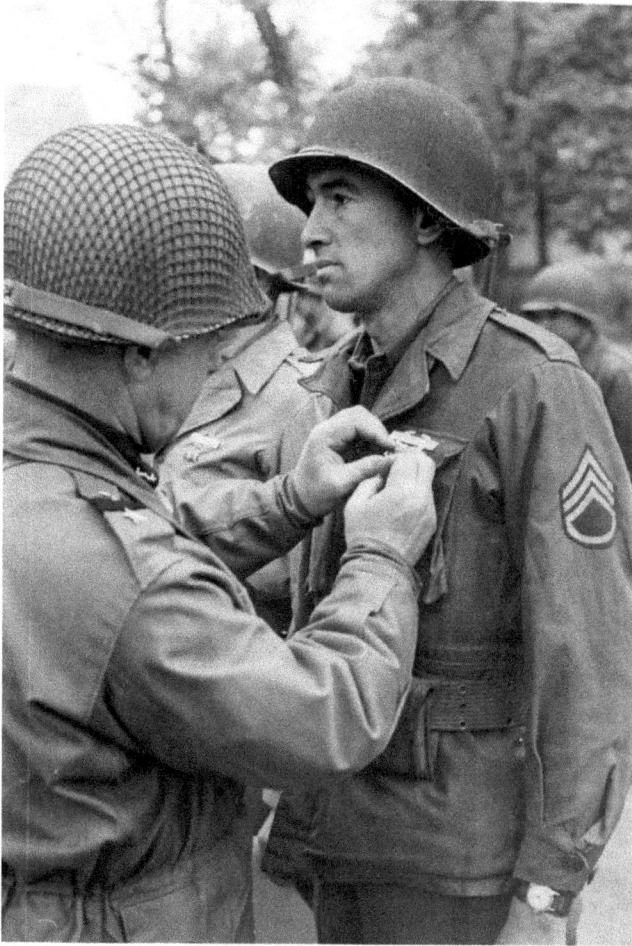

Staff Sergeant Cecil W. Rogers, from Flint Mills, Gastonia, North Carolina, was presented with the Bronze Star Medal in April of 1945 in Magdeburg, Germany, by Major General Leland S. Hobbs, commanding general of the Thirtieth Infantry Division, U.S. Army. *U.S. Army Signal Corps Photograph.*

Fork River. The property passed to John Springs, who deeded it to his son, Adam Alexander Springs. Before 1883, some called the town Spring Shoals, named for the Springs family who was said to be from Holland and came from the Dutch Colony in Queens County, New York.[129] In 1880, Rufus Y. McAden of Charlotte purchased the Springs' land on the South Fork River from W.A. and Jasper Stowe, who had acquired it sometime after Adam Springs's will was probated in 1843. The year 1881 was also the year that Springs Shoals Manufacturing Company was chartered (later the McAden and McAdenville Mills). The founders were Rufus Y. McAden and sons.[130]

Mr. George W. Ragan (1846–1936) had been a successful merchant in Lowell, North Carolina, before arriving in McAdenville to help operate the general store, and in 1890 he joined Mr. L.L. Jenkins and J.H. Craig in founding the first bank in Gaston County, the First National Bank.

Thomas A. Edison made two trips to Gaston County. During his first trip in 1884 he installed a generator in the McAden Mills located in the tiny community on the South

Fork River that later became McAdenville. He helped pave the way for Gaston County to become one of the world's major textile centers. Thomas Edison's second trip to Lincoln and Gaston Counties twenty-two years later was primarily to collect minerals for his glass tube experiments, which resulted in the first fluoroscope. He was also looking for cobalt. Edison's research would pave the way for lasers and television.

Thomas A. Edison is best remembered for inventing the electric light bulb and, fittingly, McAdenville was the home of the first light bulb in the area. People from miles away came to see this wonder. It is ironic that today McAdenville is known as "Christmas Town, USA" because of the millions of Christmas light bulbs that are turned on each year.

Cramerton

First known as Mayworth, Cramerton today is not your typical Southern small town. After visiting the downtown area, one comes away looking forward to the next visit. An aerial view shows Cramerton nestled between the graceful bend of the South Fork River and the arch of the railroad tracks. With its proximity to the river and the railroad tracks down the center of town, it could seem just like any other small Southern town, but Cramerton has a modern uniqueness to it—there are gated communities, parks and golf courses.

What in the 1800s was the Holland Farm on the river became a mill town when Stuart W. Cramer (1868–1940) laid out his plan for an ideal village. Organized in 1906 as the Maynes Manufacturing Company, the mill was enlarged in 1915. Cramer was an engineer and inventor, and pioneered advances in textile mill air conditioning. Changes took place through the years and on December 4, 1922, Cramerton Mills was formed. In 1946, the plant and town were purchased by Burlington Industries.

The town was renamed Cramerton in 1920 after having been called Mayworth for its first fourteen years. In 1946 Burlington Mills purchased the Cramerton Mills. Of interest is the Mayworth School, which is on the National Register of Historic Places.

The quiet beauty of Cramerton takes one quite by surprise as she crosses under the one-car underpass and over the bridge where the railroad, almost like a monorail, and the South Fork River run through town. And then there is "Goat Island," which the city purchased with plans for a golf course. It is amazing that Cramerton has kept its identity with Gastonia, Belmont and Charlotte crowding in on three sides.

Hardin

On maps it is usually spelled Hardin or Hardins, but in error. The community was named for Holmes Harden, president of the Chester & Lenoir Railway. It was first called Worth. Descendants of German immigrants along the northern border of Gaston County organized the Harden Manufacturing Company in 1889. The mill was built in the valley of the river, with a dam across the shoal. Two landmarks are Hardin Baptist Church and Saint Paul Lutheran Church.

Stanley

At first sight Stanley seems your quintessential small Southern town with the railroad track running down the center of town. Originally called Brevard Station, Stanley's beginning actually dates back to the 1700s and pioneer days. One of these early pioneers of upper Gaston County was Robert Alexander Brevard, who settled early in the area that later would become Stanley. When the Carolina Central Railroad decided to build through the area, Robert Brevard deeded over 167 acres of land on the condition that the town and the railroad depot carry the name of Brevard Station.

The arrival of the railroad around 1860, right before the outbreak of the Civil War, made Brevard Station a very important town in Gaston County. Dallas was still the county seat and Gastonia was only a sparsely populated town at that time. Brevard Station was the only town in Gaston County at that time to have a rail outlet, although Cherryville got an outlet very soon after Stanley.

Brevard Station did a thriving "receiving and dispatching" business. All shipments of freight for miles around were routed through Brevard Station. After the rail lines were extended from Charlotte to Brevard Station, passengers were transferred to wagons for the trip on to Lincolnton and points in western North Carolina.

Brevard Station became an important relay point for the mail, but the War Between the States is what gave it somewhat of a "boomtown" designation. It became a gathering point for Confederate soldiers from area counties. Soldiers camped in the town, recruits drilled in the streets and part of the rail station was used as a commissary. There were even threats from Union sympathizers of burning the station down because it was so important to the cause of the Confederacy.[131] Because of the existence of Brevard in the North Carolina Mountains, and to avoid confusion, the name of Brevard Station was eventually dropped in favor of Stanley Creek in 1893.

Stanley Creek had been named for prospector Colonel Stanley, who had prospected for gold on the local creek, although very little is known about him. John, George and David Stanley all lived in the area in the 1700s. Eventually Stanley Creek was shortened to Stanley in 1911.

One of the earliest pioneers in the area was German immigrant Adam Cloninger and his wife Eve Magdalene Rhyne, who was the daughter of Jacob and Elizabeth Wills Rhyne. They lived east of Stanley, near Stanley Creek, where the Cloninger-Derr Cemetery is located on Virginia Avenue off Black Snake Road. Adam served in the Revolutionary War under General Rutherford. Land was granted to him on August 7, 1787. Some of the other early settlers were the families of Hovis, Rhyne, Shetley, Nance, Stroup, Hoyle, Best (Bess), Moore, Smith, McGinnis and Lineberger.[132]

Among the men from the Stanley area who served in the Revolutionary War were Thomas Campbell, William Gregory, Jonas Bradshaw, Jacob Hoffman and William Rankin. Rankin was a prisoner of war during the war, but was eventually released. He lived to age ninety-three, and before his death he was the last surviving Revolutionary War veteran in Gaston County.[133]

Confederate veterans from the Gaston-Lincoln County area held a reunion at an old school at Stanley sometime after the turn of the century. Some are wearing Southern Crosses of Honor. *Courtesy Cherryville Historical Museum.*

Located on the Stanley-Lucia Road is a Gaston County landmark, the Rhyne House, built in 1799. The house is the oldest brick house in Gaston County. The Hoyle House is older, but of a frame construction. The house was built by Thomas Rhyne who was born in Germany in 1742.

Belmont

Belmont, at one time called Garibaldi, was not incorporated until 1895, but its history goes back to well before the Revolutionary War when pioneers came into the area where they cleared forests and established farms. Around 1750 a fort was built at the confluence of the Catawba and the South Fork Rivers by Robert Leeper and others. Soon, more Scots-Irish settlers arrived from Virginia. Much of the land that would become Belmont was acquired by the father of Major William Chronicle.[134] Major William Chronicle led his "South Fork Boys," along with the Overmountain Men, against the Loyalist troops at the Battle of Kings Mountain. Major Chronicle was killed there.

Tate's Mill at Mountain Island and Woodlawn Mill, built by Caleb Lineberger, later known as "Pinhook," were built around 1850. Stowe's Factory cotton mill on the lower South Fork River was built by the sons of Larkin Stowe in 1853.[135]

In May of 1870, Mecklenburg County voters approved a bond for railroad construction for southern expansion across the Catawba River, unwittingly securing the future of Belmont.[136] The rail bridge across the Catawba would be at the Point, and when the railway was completed in 1872, there would be a fuel stop there. That meant construction of a large water tower, wood rack and station house.[137] The engineer sent to supervise the project was John Garibaldi from Italy. This water tank and fueling station became known as Garibaldi Station, but was later renamed Belmont in honor of August Belmont, a New York banker.

In 1873, Alex Beatty built a store at the railroad's crossing of the main road through the Point. Soon Abram Stowe and others would build businesses. In 1889, Stowe and Puett Store was established (later Stowe Brothers and then Stowe Mercantile) and J.W. Armstrong built a grocery store and became postmaster.[138]

In 1876, Benedictine Monks founded a monastery that would become Maryhelp Abbey, and a school that would become Belmont Abbey College. The Sisters of Mercy established a convent and Sacred Heart School for Girls, which became Sacred Heart College. The Belmont Abbey Cathedral is on the National Register of Historic Places.

Nancy Hanks, mother of Abraham Lincoln, made her home as a young girl with her uncle, Richard (Dicky) Hanks, in a cabin overlooking the Catawba River. DNA may someday answer questions about her and her son's parentage. *Photo by Rita Wehunt-Black.*

In 1901 the Chronicle Mill and a village for workers was built. Between 1919 and 1921, seven new textile manufacturing companies were organized.

In 1991, Daniel Stowe Botanical Garden opened and remains one of the largest and most extensive gardens in the United States. In 1995, Belmont celebrated its centennial. Belmont Historical Society's Cultural & Heritage Learning Center and Museum is located at 40 East Catawba Street, Belmont.

Lucia

The Lucia community extends northward from the Mountain Island community to the Lincoln County line and westward from the Catawba River to Dutchman's Creek. Some of the old schools in the area were the Huckleberry School and Piney Grove School. There was also a Lucia teacherage. Lucia was the home of James Johnson, an officer in the American Revolution and a member of the Provincial Congress, legislature and convention of 1788. Two early churches began in Lucia: the Old Whitehaven Lutheran Church and Castanea Presbyterian Church.

Alexis

Located not far from the Lincoln County line, Alexis is a very small community in northern Gaston County. There is Alexis Post Office, and among the local churches in the area are Mount Zion Baptist Church and the Alexis Baptist Church, organized in 1903. At one time there was a cotton gin. Some of the early settlers were the families of Garrison, Stroup, Rhyne, Hoyle, Abernethy, Lineberger, Hovis and others.[139]

Boogertown and Booger Mountain

Schoolchildren once had enjoyable Easter egg hunts on Booger Mountain. Students from Victory School hiked several miles to get to the mountain. Booger Mountain has also been known as Jackson Knob and Pleasant Ridge.

Victory School Community

The Victory Community grew up around the Osceola and Seminole textile mills, owned by W.T. Rankin and C.G. Armstrong. Victory School opened around 1918. Later, the Ruby, Dixon, Winget and Victory Mills were organized, which increased the population of the area.

Lowell

Dating back to 1850, Lowell was originally known as Wright's Station. A station had been built with the coming of the Charlotte and Atlanta Air Line Railroad. The station was named for William "Bill" Wright, who was the nearest resident to the station at the time. Soon afterwards, J. Polk Glenn built a general store in the community. The post office and a bar were also located in the building. The following year, in 1873, George W. Ragan, a twenty-six-year-old South Point native, and farmer Captain Samuel J. Hand opened the second store in Lowell.[140]

The actual town of Lowell, like Bessemer City, was a planned town from the beginning. The small community already existed in 1879 when Neal Dumont arrived from Lowell, Massachusetts, and married the daughter of J. Caleb Lineberger, a well-known textile pioneer. Dumont secured the services of an engineer who laid out the town in blocks and named the streets. Great care was used in deciding on the name of Lowell for the town. The choices were Lowell or Manchester. Lowell, Massachusetts, and Manchester, England, were both large industrial centers known for their textile mills. Lowell became a shipping point between the Woodlawn Mill and Spencer Mountain Mill.

In the 1880s, Dr. Frank Robinson, the town's first doctor, opened his practice in Lowell, and George A. Gray established the first real boardinghouse in town. There was also a teacherage. After the turn of the century, several textile mills were built in Lowell and many new homes were constructed.

Today Lowell is not a major industrial center, but is a charming town, and it seems that the people of Lowell like it just the way it is.

Mount Holly

Settled mainly by Scots-Irish, Mount Holly is one of the oldest communities in Gaston County. Much of present-day Mount Holly is on land described in an old Armstrong grant from George II, transferred to George Rutledge in 1753. It was described as a parcel of land "on the south side of the Catawba River on Kuykendall, the Dutchman's Creek." Kuykendall was one of the few German settlements, in a sea of Scots-Irish settlements, in what would become northeastern Gaston County.

Gaston County's industry started with the building of the Mountain Island Mill and the Old Woodlawn Mill at nearby Tuckaseegee Ford, so at one time Mount Holly was known as Woodlawn. There was a Woodlawn Post Office; however, the railroad listed the station as Tuckaseegee Station. Some say that Mount Holly was renamed when a cotton mill was organized by brothers A.P. Rhyne and D.E. Rhyne in 1875. It was said at the time that the best yarns on the market were produced by the mills in Mount Holly, New Jersey, and it was hoped by the mill owners that their yarns would rival the best. Others relate the story of many young holly trees on the banks of Dutchman's Creek and claim that this contributed to the name of the town.

After a year of Pacific battles, sailor Robert L. Long, fireman second class, United States Navy Reserve, of Lowell (center) talks with fellow North Carolina sailors aboard a minesweeper at a repair station in the Admiralty Islands in 1945. *Official U.S. Naval Photograph.*

The building of the Mountain Island Mill in 1848 on the banks of the Catawba River, just two years after the county was chartered, brought many families to the area and promoted growth. The Old Mountain Island Mill was washed away by the Great Flood of 1916. Both it and the Woodlawn Mill were the forerunners of Gaston County's great textile industry.

Mount Holly is situated on the west bank of the Catawba River with the business district built near the river, with hills rolling down to the deep water of the river's edge. A renewal of areas near the river is underway. Bobby Black, a Mount Holly historian, has this to say about the Mount Holly of today, "This town has sometimes been called a diamond in the rough. But I think Mount Holly is a bright, shining gemstone. We need to polish it and take pride in that."[141]

Representative of those who served in World War I is this Gaston County soldier. Some soldiers would return to Gaston County and establish homes and families; some would not. *Courtesy Cherryville Historical Museum.*

High Shoals

Gaston County's northernmost town, located on the north bank of the South Fork River, High Shoals was not incorporated until 1973, but the village and community of High Shoals is much, much older. The discovery of iron ore in the area in the 1700s brought sudden growth to the region.

Fulenwider started the High Shoals Ironworks, and in the 1800s much of the manufactured iron products were being ferried down the river by flatboats to Charleston, South Carolina, for distribution. By 1880, extensive blast furnaces were in operation. A number of roller mills, powered by water, were converting the smelted iron into bars, nails, plowshares and other wrought-iron products.

High Shoals derived its name from the shoals in the South Fork River, which are among the highest in the river. The water gushing over these shoals made for excellent water power possibilities, and a group of cotton manufacturers in the 1890s became aware of these

The Episcopal church, rectory and school located on a hill above the river in the village of High Shoals can be seen in this 1910 postcard. *Courtesy of the N.C. Division of Archives and History.*

possibilities. The Carolina and North Western Railway, running between Chester, South Carolina, and Lenoir, had been constructed near the shoals some years earlier, furnishing excellent transportation.

In the later part of the nineteenth century, iron manufacturing began to decline, and through the years High Shoals changed from a mining center to a textile community.

In the 1970s, High Shoals missed out on a chance for growth when the Miller Brewing Company decided not to build a $125 million brewery there. This was just one of many industrial blows the community received. High Shoals remains a small town and a community that has survived now for over two hundred years, and it will continue to survive.

Spencer Mountain

The community of Spencer Mountain, located in central Gaston County, developed around Spencer Mountain Mill, powered by a water wheel on the South Fork River. The town lies on the north side of Spencer Mountain between the mountain and the South Fork River. The Spencer Mountain Mill was constructed in 1874 by J. Harvey Wilson of Mecklenburg

County and J.W. Moore of Augusta, Maine. The present town of Spencer Mountain was incorporated on May 21, 1963.

Spencer Mountain, elevation 679 feet, was named for Zachariah Spencer (1732–1789), a Tory-turned-Patriot during the Revolutionary War.[142] He lived on the South Fork River below one of the ridges of Spencer Mountain.[143] Zachariah's parents were Zachariah and Christine Cobb Spencer of Baltimore, Maryland. The younger Zachariah married Anne Pogue in Baltimore before coming to North Carolina in 1772. Their son John Spencer married Ann Hoffman in 1818.[144]

Spencer Mountain is the site of the old WBTV television transmitter and the site where the first commercial television signal in North Carolina was broadcast when WBTV signed on the air in 1949. The tower is no longer in use as WBTV's primary transmitter.

Decorated at Christmas, the town of Spencer Mountain is lit with thousands of lights, reflecting against the waters of the South Fork River and bouncing off Spencer Mountain, making for a beautiful sight.

Ranlo

Ranlo got its name from the first letters of the surnames of Rankin and Love. Ranlo's scenic backdrop is Spencer Mountain. Until 1963, it was known as "Ranlo Crossroads"; and the community almost lost the possibility of ever becoming a permanent town. That is because the original charter of incorporation, hurriedly drawn up in 1963 and pushed through the General Assembly, contained a clause that gave the city of Gastonia a period of fifteen years to annex Ranlo. Ranlo officials, realizing what this would mean, had the charter amended in 1965 and the fifteen-year clause was deleted.

Still, the town will never grow to any extent because it is almost completely surrounded by Gastonia and Lowell on the east, west and south. To the north lies Spencer Mountain. This has never bothered the citizens of Ranlo because they never wanted to grow into a large town. All they wanted was to keep from being annexed by Gastonia or Lowell. Before deciding to incorporate, and when annexation looked inevitable, some residents favored annexation by Lowell; others by Gastonia.[145]

Tryon and Sunnyside

In 1779 Lincoln County was formed from Tryon County, the county seat was moved to Lincolnton and the political life of Tryon community ended. The growth of the community of Tryon in northwestern Gaston County also ended. The name Tryon endured in the community and the local volunteer fire department created the unique name Tryonota Fire District, which covers most of the area between Bessemer City, Kings Mountain and Cherryville.

A mile or so up the road is Sunnyside. The residents in the area started calling the community Sunnyside after the name of a school in the area. Also in the area was Hallman School. The county moved Sunnyside School up the road a mile toward Cherryville and named it Tryon, because the school was across the road from the site of the old Tryon Court House. Sunnyside is a picturesque community with its curving road and bottomland that was once all farmland. One pioneering family is the Kiser family. Kisers have lived in the Tryon Community since 1750.

The only intrusion in the community came in the 1970s when the Lithium Corporation of America built an open-pit mine for spodumene, which is an ore of lithium.

Cherryville

Cherryville, in the northwestern part of Gaston County, is such a beloved town that, when it comes to its history, much has been lovingly written. It is hard to improve on what has been written by Reverend C.A. Linn in 1926, David P. Dellinger in the 1950s, W. Tabor Robinson, Mary Frances Mauney and Bobbie Y. Rudisill.

Private First Class Arnold A. Duncan, twenty-four, of Cherryville, North Carolina, is being awarded the Purple Heart for machine gun wounds he suffered during the invasion of France. The award was made in England in the fall of 1944. *Official U. S. Army Photograph*

Linn, in his flowery prose that was indicative of his era, wrote about a

charming little hamlet…Cherryville's panorama is more than a beautiful garden. Being the climatic medium where the mountain's apples, chestnuts, and hams meet the southland's peanuts, persimmons and yams, it is where can be grown nearest everything; and growing nearest everything makes it a potential agricultural, horticultural and floricultural Canaan… People go clear from the south to Colorado Springs to breathe her Rocky Mountain Air; when they could get more for their money to come and breathe Cherryville's balsam breezes from the Blue Ridge, and drink her icy water from the bosom of Cherry Mountains.

W.T. Robinson wrote about the geography of Cherryville,

located in the largest part of Gaston County's Panhandle section. Located on a plateau, nine miles west of Lincolnton, the city's business area is almost 1,000 feet above sea level, the high point on the Seaboard's railway line, which runs from Charlotte to Rutherford. To the northwest can be seen, on a clear day, the South Mountains, a southern range of the Blue Ridge and Appalachian Mountains. To the south and within a distance of approximately twenty miles is Crowders Mountain, named for one of the Catawba Frontier's early settlers.

A Cherryville Street scene prior to 1911 shows Main Street and the Bull Durham Tobacco advertisement. A new city hall was built in 1911 covering the advertisement until it was again uncovered in the 1990s. *Courtesy Cherryville Historical Museum Postcard Collection.*

Cherryville's main street on "Big Celebration Day" in 1916 shows a festive crowd. *Courtesy Cherryville Historical Museum.*

Every historian and genealogist discovers early that to know the history of an area and its people he must first learn about the waterways and churches and then move on to the land deeds. This holds true for the history of Cherryville, and the waterways that we start with are Indian Creek and Beaver Dam Creek. Indian Creek rises in Catawba County, flows southeast across Lincoln County, dips briefly into northwestern Gaston County and flows back into Lincoln where it meets the South Fork of the Catawba River. Beaver Dam Creek, called by early settlers simply Beaverdam, rises in northwestern Gaston County and flows northeast into the South Fork River.

On November 23, 1762, the same date that Valentine Mauney purchased 370 acres, Thomas Black bought 380 acres from Moses Moore. This land was on the south side of Indian Creek and joined Valentine Mauney's land.

Thomas Black was descended from Scots-Irish immigrants who settled first in Pennsylvania around 1750. Members of this family moved south to North Carolina. Those who came from Pennsylvania were David, Thomas, John and William Black. Thomas, John and William were brothers and, in all likelihood, David was their father. A deed dated 1757 states that David Black, a resident of Rowan County, bought land in the region of what is now Rutherford County.

Thomas Black settled in the valley near Indian Creek in a home near Valentine Mauney's house in 1762. On September 12, 1765, Thomas bought 320 acres lying on both sides of the

Above: The Cherryville Fire Station, shown in this photograph, was located on the first floor of the city hall building, which also contained a courtroom and jail. Today it houses the Cherryville Historical Museum. *Courtesy of Cherryville Historical Museum.*

Left: The Cherryville Historical Museum, at 109 East Main Street, is located on the three floors of the old city hall, built in 1911. The firetruck, courtroom and the jail can be seen at the museum. The jail is always a favorite! *Photo by Rita Wehunt-Black.*

Little Broad River, located in present-day Cleveland County. Thomas Black left his Indian Creek home and moved to the Cleveland County property, but his descendants populated much of Cherryville Township.

Ephraim Black was born in 1767 and was the son of Thomas (1741–1779) and Elizabeth Black. Around 1797, Ephraim returned from Cleveland County with his mother to the Indian Creek property that his now deceased father had bought in 1762. He built a home there overlooking Indian Creek. Along Indian Creek also lived Burrell Homesley, Joseph Homesley and Benjamin Homesley. Stephen Homesley lived in Lincoln County at the time as well. In 1790, Ephraim Abraham Black (1767–1843) married Tabitha "Doshie" Homesley (1778–1854), the daughter of Benjamin Homesley (1750–1813). Ephraim and Tabitha Black had the following children:

1. Thomas F. Black (1792–1880), married Barbara Leonhardt, then Rebeckah Stroup. Thomas F. and Rebeckah Black were the parents of John F. Black (1848–1940), who was known for building the John Black School.
2. Jemima Black (born 1793), married Michael Mauney, son of Valentine Mauney.
3. Stephen Black (1800–1856), married Elizabeth Brown (1799–1882). They were the parents of Joseph Black (1832–1923) and Benaja Black (1827–1919), whose son was Ben Black.
4. Ephraim Black Jr. (born 1802).
5. Lawson Black (born 1805).
6. Samuel (Squire) Simpson Black (1807–1882), married Anne Carpenter (1818–1856), the daughter of Jacob Carpenter.
7. William Wiley Black, married Sally Reinhardt.
8. Alfred Black (1816–1894), married Mahala Self.
9. (Dr.) Lorenzo Dow Black, (1818–1904), married Melinda Weaver.
11. Elizabeth Black (listed in will dated 1843).
12. Abel Black (listed in will dated 1843).
13. Benage Black (listed in will dated 1843).

There may have been other children.

Thomas Black and Stephen Black built homesteads along the "Old Post Road," as it was referred to in the original grant of land in 1796. Linn described this road as

> the main thoroughfare from Charlotte to Spartanburg and therefore one of the principal connections between Washington and important points in the extreme Southern States. It was to be sure no National Highway, such as graces the state of North Carolina from Virginia to South Carolina today, but it was a cleared and established passage over which it was possible to draw the slow-moving wagons and ox-carts of the early days. The name indicates, though, that the road was looked upon chiefly as the route over which there passed the fortnightly mails that were anxiously awaited all along the way by little groups of settlers, gathered to hear the belated news from the outside world.

After the Black and Mauney families settled permanently, several other pioneer families came into the area; and the settlement, which had begun along Indian Creek, began to spread south and westward into the area that was first called White Pine and later Cherryville.

Among those settlers who came before 1800 was Stephen Homesley, who settled in what is today southwest Cherryville around 1790. Stephen's son was Amos Homesley, called Squire Homesley because he was a justice of the peace. Other families were the Eaker, Beam, Carpenter, Dellinger, Heavner, Anthony, Brown, Reynolds, Kiser, Huss, Houser, Quinn, Summit and many other families.

Prior to 1852, Benaja Black's home and little store were used as a meeting place for the community. It was in Benaja Black's home that the first post office was established in 1854. Soon the little hamlet began to grow, and at the post office a lone white pine tree grew out front and people passing through began calling the little hamlet White Pine.

Henry Summit came to Cherryville in 1852 and is credited with starting the first business in town. Near where the Old Post Road crossed the Morganton (or Burke) Road, Henry Summit built his mercantile business and distillery. Summit's store later became the new meeting place for the community. Summit's store was so successful that he erected a second store called the "Long Store," because of its shape and size.

The congregation of the Rudisill Chapel AME Zion Church was photographed around 1925. The first church was built around 1896 in Cherryville and named for Calvin Rudisill. *Courtesy Cherryville Historical Museum.*

He had such a volume of trade that at times he had six or seven clerks. Michael Logan Craft worked as a clerk in Summit's second store after Craft returned from Arkansas and married Lizzie Farris.

In *Cherryville, Past and Present*, printed in 1996, Bobbie Yount Rudisill gives Henry Summit credit for helping with the start of several churches in Cherryville. She states that,

> *The first thing that impressed me was the great contribution and influence of Mr. Henry Summit in the Religious life of the community. This man gave of his facilities, his property and his family in helping to establish our churches. His granary, which stood near the corner of present day Oak and Main Streets, was used by Lutherans, Methodists, and Wesleyans for worship services. In fact, it was in that building that St. John's Lutheran and Methodist churches were organized. He donated property to the Lutherans, Methodists and Baptists for building sites.*

The lot on North Mountain Street near the present Highway 150 intersection was given to the Baptist Church by Henry Summit, but was later disposed of for a more suitable location. Joseph Black gave the property for First Baptist Church, and in his will he donated property for a cemetery on East Church Street, which today is Cherryville Memorial Cemetery. Many other businesses would follow Summit's by men named Beam, Elliot, Mauney, Rudisill, Hendricks, Aderholdt, Hobbs, McGinnis, Harrelson, Houser, Kendrick, Stroup and others. Cherryville also had one of the largest foundries in the state. Cherryville was turning into a real town. When the 1889 Census was taken, Cherryville was the fourth largest town in Gaston County with 68 citizens; Dallas was the largest with 417; Gastonia next with 236 citizens; and then Stanley with 75 citizens recorded. The charter for the town of Cherryville was granted on February 19, 1881. The first mayor of Cherryville was James C. Elliott, who had served in the Confederate army.

On February 18, 1891, industrial development came to Cherryville with the organization of the Cherryville Manufacturing Company for the purpose of opening Cherryville's first cotton mill. The Cherryville Manufacturing Company became known as the "old mill" and the neighborhood around it "the old mill hill." The Gaston Manufacturing Company, which was later sold to Dover Mills and then became known as Dora Yarn Mills, was formed in 1896, and the company built its first plant in 1897; its second plant was built in 1905. The Vivian Manufacturing Company, which later became the Nu-Way Mills, was organized on March 6, 1917; the Rhyne-Houser Manufacturing Company, in 1919; the Josephine Knitting Mills, in 1922; and the Carlton Yarn Mills, in 1922.

What would grow into one of the nation's largest freight carriers started operating in Cherryville in 1933 as Beam Trucking Company. C. Grier Beam and his brother D.F. Beam, and what would become Carolina Freight, did as much to change the economy and the face of Cherryville as the cotton mills had done earlier in Cherryville's history.

Noah Benjamin Kendrick of Cherryville built this house, designed by Hugh White, in 1922 as a showplace for the use of Kendrick Brick and Tile. Today a Gaston County Historic Property, it is owned by Helen H. Lamoureux. *Courtesy Cherryville Historical Museum.*

Kings Mountain

Yes, Kings Mountain, once known as White Plains, is actually located in two counties. Today approximately eight hundred citizens, out of around ten thousand, live in Gaston County.

Bessemer City

Bessemer City is located at the foot of Whetstone Mountain in the western section of Gaston County. The area's first settlers beginning in the 1750s were miners, lumbermen and farmers. Iron mining and smelting was prevalent in the area long before there was a town. James Ormand, John Fulenwider and others produced some of the highest-quality iron ore in America. When John Fulenwider died in 1826, he owned over twenty thousand acres in the Bessemer City region.[146] The town got its name from Sir Henry Bessemer, who invented the "Bessemer Process" for mass producing steel from iron ore.

In 1871, the Atlanta & Charlotte Division of the Richmond & Danville Railroad Company laid track through Whetstone Mountain, located to the west of Bessemer City. The railroad stimulated growth in the area and in 1893, John Askew Smith, wife Fanny

Grier Beam was inducted posthumously into the North Carolina Transportation Hall of Fame in 2007. He started Carolina Freight Corporation in 1932 in this Shell Station. Listed on the National Register of Historic Places, it houses a truck museum. *Courtesy Cherryville Museum.*

September 15, 1917, the first World War I servicemen to leave Cherryville. *Front*: Sid Carpenter, Earl Costner, Jim Black, Webb Eaker and Gus Mauney. *Back*: John Whitworth, I.P. Long, Tom Self, Gyser Canipe, unknown and Arthur Dellinger. *Courtesy of Cherryville Historical Museum.*

and brother-in-law John A. Pinchback from Reidsville, moved to the area. Smith purchased seventeen hundred acres to establish a town on the east side of Whetstone Mountain. Smith hired W.R. Richardson, an engineer from Guilford County, to lay out the town. A lot of the streets in Bessemer City are named after states—there is Pennsylvania Avenue, Virginia Avenue, Maryland Avenue and other interesting street names.

By 1893, Smith and other residents petitioned the North Carolina legislature to incorporate the town, and on March 6, 1893, Bessemer City was officially chartered. By 1900, the population had grown to six hundred people. The Bessemer City Cotton Mill was organized, and later the Whetstone Mill in 1905. Smith and Pinchback erected the initial building that housed the Osage Manufacturing Company.

This picture is signed on the back: "Lovingly, Lizzie Michume 'The Original' Bessemer City, N.C." Several of these pictures have been found in Gaston County—one says it was donated by "Mrs. Jno. E. Jones," but nothing more is known. *Courtesy Cherryville Museum.*

Dellview

Dellview lies in the far northwestern section of Gaston County. It was founded by J.H. Dellinger and Tom Dellinger in 1924. It is the smallest incorporated town in the United States with a population always less than twenty. The original purpose for incorporating Dellview was to get electricity brought to the area; some say it was founded because a local ordinance would not allow the control of wild dogs that were killing chickens.

Another interesting fact about Dellview is that it is said to be approximately the midpoint between Atlanta, Georgia, and Washington, D.C., and it was used as a reference point for pilots during the 1920s, 1930s and 1940s.

The Panhandle of Gaston County

A geographical term that has all but died out in Gaston County is "the Panhandle" area. When looking at a map of Gaston County, the northwestern corner is in the shape of the handle of a pan, with the rest of the county being the pan. Originally, the "Panhandle" referred to the area of Cherryville, along with all the other land lying west of Cherryville to the Lincoln and Cleveland County lines, including what today is Dellview.

The Mount Zion Baptist Church congregation in the year 1910. *Courtesy Cherryville Historical Museum.*

The children of John Charles and Catherine Sprott Carpenter: Clarence Eugene Carpenter (1873–1966), who married Gaddie Lee Harrelson, sits with his sister, Nancy Jane Sprott Carpenter (1876–1967), wife of Charles Lester Beam. *Courtesy Cherryville Historical Museum.*

On some early census records this area is called Craigeville. The area has a distinct history and today it is usually referred to as the Mount Zion area, the Flint Hill area or Hugh's Pond area. Originally, the families in this area included the Carpenters, Crafts, Harrelsons, Blacks, Dellingers, Fishers, Mitchems Mosses, Helms, Eakers, Stroups, Anthonys, Putnams, Whites, Morrisons and many others.

One of the oldest Baptist churches in Gaston County, Mount Zion Baptist Church, is located in the panhandle. Mount Zion Baptist Church celebrated its 150th anniversary in October of 2007. This vicinity has probably been a place of worship for over two hundred years. On May 8, 1807, Benjamin Anthony, Nicholas Ayers and Jacob Dellinger, trustees for the congregation belonging to Anthony's Meeting House (an interdenominational meetinghouse) in the county of Lincoln (today Gaston) and along the waters of Indian Creek on the Burke Road leading from Morganton to Charleston, near the Flint Hill Road, sold for one dollar land for use as a church and Presbyterian meetinghouse. Between 1807 and 1856, the name was changed to Hebron Meeting House. Around this same time, Lutherans and Presbyterians left Hebron Meeting House.

In 1856 various Baptists living in the vicinity of Hebron Meeting House purchased a tract of land for the purpose of building a Baptist Church, and on October 7, 1857, a Baptist Church was organized and given the name Mount Zion. The charter members were Moses Evans, F.L. Dellinger, T.H. Mullinax, Isom White, Robert Morrison, D.F. Stroup, Alfred Black, Phillip Dellinger, Samuel Dellinger, Wiley Runnels, Samuel Barnhill, Peter Dellinger, Daniel Morrison, Thomas Black, L.L. McGinnis, W.H. Putnam, P.A. Proctor, Daniel Summitt, E.R. Wellmon,

The John F. Black School was located two miles north of Cherryville and was built around 1897; it closed in 1913. *Courtesy Cherryville Historical Museum.*

Luesa Runnels, Mary Dellinger, Mrs. Jane White, Susan Runnels, Nancy E. Stroup, Sarah Evans, Fanny Brown, Jane Neel, Margaret Dellinger, Margaret Ann Stroup, Mary Wellmon, Nancy Griggs, Rosanes Morrison, Lucinda Black, Julian Mullinax, Caroline Dellinger, Sarah M. Summitt, Fenetta Wellmon and Miss Jane White.

The Mount Zion congregation first met in a "brush arbor" near Indian Creek, and then moved into Anthony's Meeting House. In 1858, the first church was built. This church was located near the present-day church, where a community cemetery had already been started; but it was not until soldiers returned from the Civil War that the interior of the church was finished. The congregation used this structure until it was destroyed by fire in 1902.

The next church building was built under the leadership of Reverend D.F. Putnam around 1902.

Mount Zion was the moving spirit in the organization of many other churches in the area; among them are First Baptist Church of Cherryville, Leonard's Fork Baptist, Pleasant Grove Baptist and Shady Grove Baptist.

The schools in the area were the Black Rock School, Gray Rock School, the Panhandle School and the John F. Black School. John F. Black (1848–1940) was the son of Thomas Black and his wife, Rebeckah Stroup.

Above: Pictured are members of Saint Paul's Methodist Church Ladies Aid Society around 1928. They all lived in the panhandle area of Gaston County. Members of the Craft, Harrelson, Baxter and Moss families are represented. *Courtesy Cherryville Historical Museum*

Left: David Andrew Craft (1857–1958) was a prominent citizen of the panhandle section. He died at the age of one hundred, leaving many descendants. The first documented Craft in Lincoln County is Michael Craft, born in 1754. *Courtesy Cherryville Historical Museum.*

Notes

PREFACE

1. Kate Wolf, "Across the Great Divide," *Gold in California*, CD (Los Angeles, CA: Rhino Records, 1980).

THE LAY OF THE LAND

2. Dr. Alan May, *An Archaeological Reconnaissance of Selected Portions of Gaston County, North Carolina* (Gastonia, NC: Schiele Museum of National History, 1985).
3. For more information about the Gaston County Inventory, visit the North Carolina Natural Heritage Program at their website www.http://ncnhp.org.
4. May, *Arch. Recon.*
5. Walter C. Biggs, and James F. Parnell, *State Parks of North Carolina* (Winston-Salem, NC: John F. Blair, 1989).
6 Henry J. Savage, Elizabeth Savage, Daniel Stowe Botanical Gardens, *André and Francois André Michaux* (Charlottesville: The University Press of Virginia, 1986).
7. To learn more about Daniel J. Stowe (1913–2006), the founder of the gardens who most people associate with textiles, read Daniel J. Stowe, By Waters of the South Fork (Charlotte, NC: Laney-Smith, 2000).

THE SCOTS-IRISH AND THE CAROLINA BACKCOUNTRY

8. David Hackett Fisher, *Albion's Seed: Four British Folkways in America* (New York: Oxford University Press, 1989), 759.
9. John A. Lawson, and Hugh Talmadge Lefler, ed. *A New Voyage to Carolina (London 1709)*, (Chapel Hill: University of North Carolina Press, 1967).
10. Ibid.
11. Ross Yockey, *Between Two Rivers* (Belmont, NC: Sally Hill McMillan & Associates, 1996), 1.
12. Bruce Henderson, *The Charlotte Observer*, November 2007, 10-A.
13. Ibid., 7.
14. Minnie Stowe Puett, *History of Gaston County* (Charlotte, NC: Charlotte Printing, 1939), 41.
15. Ibid., 42.
16. Ibid.

17. Ibid.
18. Ibid., 44.

PATHFINDERS, PIONEERS AND PATRIOTS

19. Gaston County Historic Preservation Commission: Mrs. Richard Penegar, Robert Carpenter, Mrs. W.N. Craig, Mrs. Gerald Deal, Mike Peters, John Russell, H.O. Williams, David Williams, *Proposal of Tryon Courthouse Site: The Gaston County Historic Properties* (July 2004).
20. David Crass, Stephen Smith, Martha Zierden, and Richard Brooks, eds., *The Southern Colonial Backcountry* (Knoxville: The University of Tennessee Press, 1998), 80–81.
21. "Tryon County North Carolina Court Minutes, 1769–79," July 1770.
22. Parke Rouse Jr., *The Great Wagon Road*. (Richmond, VA: The Dietz Press, Reprint 2004), 177.
23. "Anson County Deed Abstracts," 1749–1757, p. 47.
24. "Anson County, NC Deeds," Book 6, p. 412.
25. *Colonial Records of North Carolina*, Vol. 5, pp. 604–605.
26. Ibid., Vol. 5, p. 694.
27. Miles S. Philbeck, *Mecklenburg County, North Carolina Land Index, 1763–1768*, 1988.
28. Griffin, Clarence W., *History of Old Tryon and Rutherford Counties North Carolina, 1730–1936* (Spartanburg, SC: Reprint Co., 1937).
29. Mecklenburg County, NC, Land Deeds.
30. Linda Moore Bollinger, *The Leading Edge: A History of the Family of Aaron Moore* (Irving, TX: Self-published, 1993).
31. Ibid.
32. Ibid.
33. Lyman Copeland Draper, Anthony Allair, and Isaac Shelby, *King's Mountain and Its Heroes* (Cincinnati, OH: P.G. Thomson, 1881).
34. Bollinger, *Leading Edge*.
35. John H. Wheeler, *Historical Sketches of North Carolina to 1851* (Philadelphia, Pennsylvania: 1851).
36. Draper, et al., *King's Mountain*, 298.
37. Notes by James Havilah Gordon, a descendant of Moses Moore.
38. Public Laws of North Carolina 1846–1847, 24, 25.

IRON FURNACES AND GOLD IN GASTON COUNTY

39. Ibid., 31.
40. Reverend Ben F. Ormand, *Ormand History and Decendants of James Ormand, Sr.* (Greenville, SC: A Press, Inc., 1983), 29.
41. Ibid.
42. Ibid., 30.
43. Ibid., 31.
44. Cyrus Lee Hunter, *Sketches of North Carolina History, Historical and Biographical* (Raleigh, NC: The Raleigh News Steam Job Print, 1877; The Edwards and Broughton Company, Reprint 1930), 222–223.
45. Ormand, *Ormand History*, 12.
46. Ibid., 33.
47. Robert F. Cope, and Manly Wade Wellman, *The County of Gaston: Two Centuries of a North Carolina Region* (Gastonia: Gaston County Historical Society, 1961), 72.
48. Ibid.

49. Ibid., 111.

50. William L. Sherrill, *Annals of Lincoln County, North Carolina* (Charlotte, NC: N.p., 1937), 442.

51. *Gastonia Gazette*, October 1946; Marjorie W. Young, and L.P. Walker, *Textile Leaders of the South* (Columbia, SC: The R.L. Bryan Company, 1963).

52. Dave Baity, *Tracks Through Time: A History of the City of Kings Mountain 1874–2005.* Charlotte, NC: Jostens Books, 2005), 11.

53. Ibid.

54. Catherine W. Bishir & Michael T. Southern, *A Guide to the Historic Architecture of Piedmont North Carolina* (Chapel Hill: The University of North Carolina Press, 2003).

55. Ibid.

56. Richard F. Knapp. *Golden Promise in the Piedmont: The Story of John Reed's Mine.* (Raleigh, NC: North Carolina Division of Archives and History, 1999), 3-4.

57. John Hairr and Joey Powell, *Gold Mines in North Carolina* (Charleston, SC: Arcadia Publishing, 2004).

58. North Carolina Geological Survey Brochure.

59. Ibid.

60. Ibid.

61. Ibid., 7.

62. Cope & Wellman, *The County*, 59.

63. K.W. Brengle, *The Architectural Heritage of Gaston County* (Gastonia, NC: Commercial Printers, 1982).

64. Ibid.

65. Ibid.

66. Chip Johnson, *Gaston Observer*, April 15, 2007, 6L.

67. Ibid.

Taking the Waters

68. Crowders Mountain State Park Museum.

69. Ibid.

70. Vol. 51, 68–97.

71. Crowders Mountain State Park Museum.

72. Ibid.

73. Ibid.

74. Ibid.

75. Ibid.

76. Ibid.

77. "The Lilac & the Apple" from Wolf, *Gold*.

78. *The Bessemer City Record*, March 1975.

79. Hilda Gunst, "Early Times," *Bessemer City Centennial, 1893–1993*, (Bessemer City, NC: Walsworth Publishing Company, 1993), 1.

80. Ibid.

81. Ibid.

82. Joseph H. Separk, *Gastonia and Gaston County, North Carolina 1846–1949: Past, Present, Future* (Kingsport, TN: Kingsport Press, 1936), 163.

83. *Prospectus of the Bessemer City Mining and Manufacturing Company* (Richmond, VA: Baughman Stationery Co., 1891). Pamphlet Collection, Duke University Library.

84. Ibid.

85. Ibid.

86. Ibid.
87. Ibid.
88. "Anson County, NC Deed Abstracts, 1749–1757," p. 47.

THE GERMAN MIGRATION

89. Dr. Arta F. Johnson, "Emigration from the German States," *The Palatine Immigrant* Vol. XXIX, No.3, (June 2004): 3–4.
90. Tyler Blethen, and Curtis Wood Jr., *From Ulster to Carolina* (Western Carolina University: The Mountain Heritage Center, 1983, 1986).
91. Jan A. Bankert, *Digges Choice 1724–1800: A History of Land Transactions within a portion of York and Adams County, Pennsylvania* (Rockport, ME: Picton Press, 1995).
92. James L. Haney Jr., *Stumbling Toward Zion: A Mosteller Chronicle* (Moorhead, MN: Sorbie Tower Press, 1991), 98–99
93. Ibid., 100.
94. Ibid., 101.
95. Wilma A. Dunnaway, *Pressures Toward Assimilation of European Ethnic Groups*, Electronic Archives, p. 2.
96. Morton Montgomery, *History of Berks County, Pennsylvania* (Philadelphia: Everts, Peck and Richards, 1886).
97. R. Edward Wright, *Adams County Church Records of the 18th Century*, Colonial Roots, (Lewes, DE: Colonial Roots, 1989), 65.
98. William Powell, *North Carolina through Four Centuries* (Chapel Hill: The University of North Carolina Press, 1989), 109.
99. Ibid., 110.
100. Vol. II, 1066.
101. Edward Miller Fogel, *Beliefs and Superstitions of the Pennsylvania Germans* (Millersville, Pennsylvania: Center for Pennsylvania German Studies, Millersville University, 1915, 2nd rev. ed. 1995), 208.
102. Minnie Stowe Pruett, *History of Gaston County* (Charlotte, NC: Laney-Smith, 1998), 48.
103. G.D. Bernheim, *History of the German Settlements and of the Lutheran Church in North and South Carolina* (Philadelphia: The Lutheran Book Store, 1872), 440–441.

CHILD LABOR AND MILL STRIKES

104. Vincent J. Roscigno, and William F. Danaher, *The Voice of Southern Labor* (Minneapolis: University of Minnesota Press, 2004), ix, xv.
105. Ibid., xv.
106. Ibid., 78.
107. Ibid., 89.
108. Ibid., 18–19.

IT TAKES A (MILL) VILLAGE

109. Jacquelyn Dowd Hall, et al., *Like A Family: the Making of a Southern Cotton Mill World* (Chapel Hill: University of North Carolina Press, 1987), 114.
110. Ibid., 179.
111. Liston Pope, *Millhands and Preachers* (New Haven, CT: Yale University Press, 1942), 126–140.
112. Ibid., 44.
113. Hall, *Like a Family*, 114.

114. *Gastonia Gazette*, April 26, 1980.
115. Gaston County Heritage Book Committee, *Gaston County Heritage Book* (Lincolnton, NC: Gaston County Heritage Book Committee, 2002), 288.
116. Roscigno & Danaher, *The Voice*, 80.
117. Ibid., 52.
118. Daniel J. Stowe, *By Waters of the South Fork* (Charlotte, NC: Laney-Smith, 2000), 25.
119. Ibid., 25.
120. Ibid., 26.
121. *Gastonia Gazette*, April 30, 1977.
122. *The Cherryville Eagle*, October 4, 1972.
123. Cherryville History Committee: Von Eva Allran, Bill Carpenter, Gert Fisher, Bobbie Rudisill, Camilla Young, *Cherryville Past & Present 1996* (Cherryville, NC: Ken Rollins Printer & Publisher, 1996), 6.
124. Ibid., 19.

Towns and Communities in Gaston County

125. Cope & Wellman, *The County*, 150.
126. *Gastonia Gazette*, April 24, 1976.
127. Billy Robert Miller, *McAdenville: Spun from the Wilderness* (Charlotte, NC: Laney-Smith, 2000), 31–32.
128. *Gastonia Daily Gazette*, Oct. 5, 1946
129. Ibid.
130. Miller, *McAdenville*, 30.
131. *Gastonia Gazette*, April 30, 1977; April 26, 1980.
132. Jim Hefner, "A Place Called Home," "Stanley," *The King's Mountain Herald*, November 21, 2007, 3.
133. Ibid.
134. Ross Yockey, *Between Two Rivers* (Charlotte, NC: City of Belmont, and Sally Hill McMillan and Associates, Inc., 1996), 191.
135. Ibid.
136. Ibid., 23.
137. Ibid.
138. Ibid., 193.
139. Heritage Book Committee, *Gaston County Heritage Book*, "Grace Maxwell & Sara Grissop," 216–217.
140. Ibid., "Robert A. Ragan," 286–287.
141. Thomas Lark, "Mount Holly: Historic Past, Bright Future," *The King's Mountain Herald*, November 21, 2007, 9.
142. Heritage Book Committee, *Gaston County Heritage Book*, "Mary Anne Spencer Goodman," 187.
143. Ibid., "Charlotte Isbill," 288.
144. Ibid., "Mary Anne Spencer Goodman," 187.
145. *Gastonia Gazette*, April 1977
146. *Bessemer City Centennial 1893–1993*.

Selected Bibliography

Aheron, Piper Peters. *Images of America: Gastonia and Gaston County, North Carolina.* Charleston, SC: Arcadia Publishing Company, 2001.

Baity, Dave. *Tracks Through Time: A History of the City of Kings Mountain 1874–2005.* Charlotte, NC: Jostens Books, 2005.

Bernheim, G.D. *History of the German Settlements and of the Lutheran Church in North and South Carolina.* Philadelphia: The Lutheran Book Store, 1872.

Bishir, Catherine W., and Michael T. Southern. *A Guide to the Historic Architecture of Piedmont North Carolina.* Chapel Hill: University of North Carolina Press, 2003.

Blethen, Tyler, and Curtis Wood Jr. *From Ulster to Carolina: The Migration of the Scotch-Irish to Southwestern North Carolina.* Western Carolina University: The Mountain Heritage Center, 1983, 1986.

Bollinger, Linda Moore. *The Leading Edge: A History of the Family of Aaron Moore, Pennsylvania Indian Trader and North Carolina Pioneer.* Irving, TX: Self-published, 1993.

Brengle, K.W. *The Architectural Heritage of Gaston County.* Gastonia, NC: Commercial Printers, 1982.

Bryson, Herman J. *Gold Deposits in North Carolina.* Raleigh: North Carolina Department Of Conservation and Development, 1936.

Burgert, Annette K. *York County Pioneers From Friedelsheim and Gonnheim in the Palatinate.* Worthington, OH: AKB Publications, 1984.

Carpenter, P.A. III. *Gold Resources of North Carolina.* Raleigh: North Carolina Department of Natural Resources and Community Development, 1972.

Carpenter, Robert C. *Carpenters A Plenty.* Baltimore, MD: Gateway Press, Inc., 1982.

———. *The History of Bethel Evangelical Lutheran Church.* Bethel Evangelical Lutheran Church Celebration Committee, 2000.

Carson, Paul. *Overmountain Victory National Historic Trail: A Progress report on the Status of the Trail.* Blacksburg, SC: National Park Service, Winter 2005.

Cope, Robert F., and Manly Wade Wellman. *The County of Gaston: Two Centuries of a North Carolina Region.* Gastonia: Gaston County Historical Society, 1961.

Corbitt, David L. *The Formation of the North Carolina Counties 1663–1943*. Raleigh, NC: State Department of Archives and History, 1950.

Crass, David Colin, Steven D. Smith, Martha A. Zierden, and Richard D. Brooks, eds. *The Southern Colonial Backcountry: Interdisciplinary Perspectives on Frontier Communities*. Knoxville: The University of Tennessee Press, 1998.

Davenport, Douglas. "A History of Linwood College." Unpublished thesis, Appalachian State Teachers College, 1959.

Fisher, David Hackett. *Albion's Seed*. New York: Oxford University Press, 1989.

Gaston County Heritage Book Committee. *Gaston County Heritage*, Vol. 1. Winston-Salem, NC: Jostens, 2002.

Goodnight, Jerry A., and Richard Eller. *The Tarheel Lincoln: North Carolina Origins of "Honest" Abe*. Hickory, NC: Tarheel Press, 2003.

Griffin, Clarence W. *History of Old Tryon and Rutherford Counties North Carolina, 1730–1936*. Spartanburg, SC: Reprint Co., 1937.

Griffin, Sally. *Gaston Remembers: Weaving a Tapestry of Time*. Community Communications-Book Division, 1994.

Hall, Jacquelyn, James Leloudis, Robert Korstad, Mary Murphy, Lu Ann Jones and Christopher Daly. *Like A Family: The Making of a Southern Cotton Mill World*. Chapel Hill: The University of North Carolina Press, 1987.

Handsel, Joyce J., Sarah H. Grissop, and Stanley Historical Society. *Echoes and Shadows of Two Centuries*. Winston-Salem, NC: Jostens Graphics, 1999.

Hooker, Richard J. *The Carolina Backcountry on the Eve of Revolution: The Journal and Other Writings of Charles Woodmason*. Chapel Hill: University of North Carolina Press, 1953.

Hunter, Cyrus Lee. *Sketches of Western North Carolina, Historical and Biographical*. Raleigh, NC: The Edward and Broughton Company, Raleigh News Steam Job Print, 1877, 1930.

Knapp, Richard F. *Golden Promise in the Piedmont: The Story of John Reed's Gold Mine*. Raleigh: North Carolina Division of Archives and History, 1999.

Marino, Thomas J. *Pasour, Paysour, Payseur, Paseur, Together...at Last*. Birmingham, AL: Birmingham Publishing Company, 1992.

Mauney, Mary Frances, and Rev. John D. Mauney Jr. *Beaver Dam Lutheran Church Cemetery "A Challenge for Our Time."* Cherryville, NC: John D. Mauney Jr., 1992.

May, Alan J., and Schiele Museum of Natural History. *An Archaeological Reconnaissance of Selected Portions of Gaston County, North Carolina*. Gastonia: National Park Service, North Carolina Division of Archives and History, 1985.

May, Alan J. *Natural Heritage Inventory of Gaston County*. North Carolina Natural Heritage Program. Division of Parks and Recreation. Department of Environment and Natural Resources. Gaston County Quality of Natural Resources Commission. N.C. Cooperative Extension. December 2000.

———. "Taking the Waters: All Healing Springs Spa and Nineteenth Century Homeopathy." *North Carolina Archaeology* 51 (2002): 68–97.

Miller, Billy Robert. *McAdenville: Spun From the Wilderness*. Gastonia, NC: The E.P. Press, 1982.

"More on Nancy Hanks Lincoln Research." *The Gaston County Historical Bulletin*, Vol. 45, No. 2. Gastonia, NC: Gaston County Historical Association, 1999.

Morgan, Jacob L., Bachman S. Brown Jr., and John Hall. *History of the Lutheran Church in North Carolina*. United Evangelical Lutheran Synod of America, 1953.

Ormand, Ben F., Jr. *Ormand History and Descendants of James Ormand, Sr. 1669–1766*. Greenville, SC: A Press, 1983.

Penegar, Lucy, Robert Carpenter, David Williams, Mrs. W.N. Craig, Mrs. Gerald Deal, Mike Peters, John Russell, and H.O. Williams. *Proposal of 1901 Loray Mill Building to: The Gaston County Historic Properties*. Gastonia, NC: Gaston County Preservation Commission, 2004.

Pope, Liston. *Millhands and Preachers: A study of Gastonia*. New Haven, CT: Yale University Press, 1942, 1971.

Powell, John, and Joey Powell. *Images of America: Gold Mines in North Carolina*. Charleston, SC: Arcadia Publishing, 2004.

Powell, William S. *The North Carolina Gazetteer*. Chapel Hill: The University of North Carolina Press, 1968.

Puett, Minnie Stowe. *History of Gaston County*. Charlotte, NC: Observer Printing, 1939.

Ragan, Robert Allison. *The Ragans of Gastonia 1790–1995*. Charlotte, NC,: R.A. Ragan and Co., 1995.

Roscigno, Vincent J., and William F. Danaher. *The Voice of Southern Labor*, Vol. 19. Minneapolis: University of Minnesota Press, 2004.

Rouse, Parke, Jr. *The Great Wagon Road: From Philadelphia to the South*. Richmond, VA: Dietz Press, 1973, 2004.

Salmond, John A. *Gastonia 1929: The Story of the Loray Mill Strike*. Chapel Hill: University of North Carolina Press, 1995.

Separk, Joseph H. *Gastonia and Gaston County, North Carolina 1846–1949: Past, Present, Future*. Kingsport, TN: Kingsport Press, 1936.

Stowe, Daniel J. *By Waters of the South Fork*. Charlotte, NC: Laney-Smith, Inc., 2000.

Summer, Bonnie Mauney. *Three Mauney Families*. King's Mountain, NC: N.p., 1967.

U.S. Department of Agriculture, Natural Resources Conservation Services. *Soil Survey of Gaston County, North Carolina*. 1989.

Williams, Robert L. *Gaston County: A Pictorial History*. Norfolk, VA.: Donning Company, 1981.

Young, James R. *Textile Leaders of the South*. Columbia, SC: The R.L. Bryan Company, 1963.

Yockey, Ross. *Between Two Rivers*. Belmont, NC: Sally Hill McMillan & Associates, Inc. for City of Belmont, 1996.

Index

Visit us at
www.historypress.net